Game Design Deep Dive: F2P

Game Design Deep Dive: Free-to-Play (F2P) continues the series' focus on examining genres with a look at the history and methodology behind free-to-play and mobile games. The genre is one of the most lucrative and controversial in the industry. Josh Bycer not only lays out the potential and pitfalls of this design but also explores the ethics behind good and bad monetization.

This book offers:

- A comprehensive look at the practices behind the most popular free-to-play and mobile games
- A detailed talk about the ethics of F2P, and one of the few honest looks at it from both sides of the argument
- A perfect read for designers, students, or people wanting to educate themselves about the practices of the genre

Joshua Bycer is a Game Design Critic with more than seven years of experience critically analyzing game design and the industry itself. In that time, through Game-Wisdom.com, he has interviewed hundreds of game developers and members of the industry about what it means to design video games.

Game Design Deep Dive

Free-to-Play

Joshua Bycer

CRC Press
Taylor & Francis Group
Boca Raton London New York

CRC Press is an imprint of the
Taylor & Francis Group, an **informa** business

First edition published 2023
by CRC Press
6000 Broken Sound Parkway NW, Suite 300, Boca Raton, FL 33487-2742

and by CRC Press
4 Park Square, Milton Park, Abingdon, Oxon, OX14 4RN

CRC Press is an imprint of Taylor & Francis Group, LLC

© 2023 Joshua Bycer

ISBN: 9781032207629 (hbk)
ISBN: 9781032207612 (pbk)
ISBN: 9781003265115 (ebk)

DOI: 10.1201/9781003265115

Typeset in Minion
by Deanta Global Publishing Services, Chennai, India

Contents

Preface

Welcome to the fourth book in the *Game Design Deep Dive* series. I'm very proud of this book, not only being my longest design piece to date but also the chance to share my thoughts on ethical game design – a topic that is sorely needed in the industry. With each entry in this series, I feel that I'm improving at analyzing designs and I hope that people are getting something useful out of them.

By talking about ethics in this book, I also hope to expel the myth surrounding "stupid game designers." The notion that because a game is designed in a specific way, that it's the developers who are being dumb for making a game like that. There's a tendency when joking about systems or design to ignore the meaning and methodology about it. Part of the reason for the breakdown and exploitation with mobile games was that developers and parents alike were ignoring the impact of the market. Mechanics and systems are not inherently good or bad, or smart or stupid; it's all about the implementation and why understanding game design matters.

Acknowledgments

For each one of my books, I run a donation incentive for acknowledgments in my books. Here are the people who helped support me while I was writing *Game Design Deep Dive: Roguelikes*:

- Michael Berthaud
- Ben Bishop
- D.S
- Jason Ellis
- Jake Everitt
- Thorn Falconeye
- Puppy Games
- Luke Hughes
- Adriaan Jansen
- Jonathan Ku
- Robert Leach
- Aron Linde
- Josh Mull
- NWDD
- Rey Obomsawin
- Janet Oblinger
- Onslaught
- David Pittman
- David White

Social Media Contacts

Email: Josh@game-wisdom.com

My YouTube channel where I post daily design videos and developer interview: youtube.com/c/game-wisdom

Main site: Game-Wisdom.com

My Twitter handle: Twitter.com/GWBycer

Additional Books

If you enjoyed this entry and want to learn more about design, you can read my other works:

- *20 Essential Games to Study* – A high-level look at 20 unique games that are worth studying their design to be inspired by or for a historical look at the game industry.
- *Game Design Deep Dive: Platformers* – The first entry in the *Game Design Deep Dive* series focusing on 2D and 3D platformer design. A top–to–bottom discussion of the history, mechanics, and design of the game industry's most recognizable and long-lasting genre.
- *Game Design Deep Dive: Roguelikes* – The second entry in the *Game Design Deep Dive* series focusing on the rise and design of roguelike games. A look back at how the genre started, what makes the design unique, and an across-the-board discussion on how it has become the basis for new designs by modern developers.
- *Game Design Deep Dive: Horror* – The third entry in the *Game Design Deep Dive* series examining the philosophy and psychology behind horror. Looking at the history of the genre, I explored what it means to create a scary game or use horror elements in any genre.

The Goal of *Game Design Deep Dive: Free-to-Play*

1.1 Introduction

With the previous entry *Game Design Deep Dive: Horror* focusing on horror design, I spoke about how the genre was one of the hardest to write about due to its focus on psychology over **mechanics**. With this one, I'm now taking an eye toward a more recent genre: one that has attracted many developers and publishers with the allure of a huge payday, and one that is hard to talk about in its own way.

Free-to-play (**F2P**) design is the first genre I'm covering for this series that has a lot of negative connotations surrounding it due to many developers building exploitative and unethical systems. The term "**pay to win**" (or **P2W**) has become synonymous with the dark side of F2P, leading many consumers to automatically forsake a game (fig 1.1). When the mobile scene exploded in the late 2000s, there was another backlash toward mobile games and consumers from people who felt that they were just abusive systems and "not a real game."

DOI: 10.1201/9781003265115-1

Figure 1.1

Let's start this book off right with an exciting dopamine-boosting scene.

Besides examining the elements of each genre, another goal of the *Game Design Deep Dive* series is to explain that mechanics and systems are just tools that a developer can use. Free-to-play design is not automatically unethical or "evil"; it's all dependent on how the systems are used and built.

1.2 Consumer and Developer Benefits

A new section I'm going to start adding to the GDDD series is talking about the benefits and major points that you are going to get by reading this. Besides the historical appeal of learning how the F2P genre has grown, this entry is going to have important information for both consumers and developers.

For consumers reading this, I hope to provide you with a "survival guide" on how to look at F2P games regardless of the platform. Just as there are many people who will say that all F2P games are bad, there is not a lot of credible information for consumers in terms of how these games are designed, the methodology of their systems, and what to watch out for with unethical elements. In Chapter 9, I'm going to be talking specifically about unethical F2P systems and how to spot these red flags in the games you play, or the ones your children or family members are playing. I want to provide you with a framework for what can make a game ethical and a goal for developers to try and reach with their designs.

Understanding what is and isn't ethical F2P design is important for developers reading this. Defining a game as pay to win is not black and white – there are different degrees based on how the systems are utilized and balanced. If you're trying to compete in the space today, you need to understand what the current market is willing to accept and what systems are not being used anymore. Good F2P design doesn't mean only having great gameplay or lots of **monetization**,

Figure 1.2

Amazing examples of free-to-play games have gone on to become huge successes and studio defining titles.

but an effective balance between the two (fig 1.2). The future of the entire genre is in question at the time of writing this book, as governments around the world are taking a closer look at how these games are earning money and whether that is causing harm to the consumers. If you're not careful about your design, your game may end up on the list of games not allowed to be sold anymore.

2

The Birth of Live Service

2.1 A Brief Look at MMOGs

What would become the basis for **live service** and F2P design began with the massively multiplayer online game (**MMOG**) genre. The whole history and structure of the genre are too vast to get into for this book. The MMOG genre originally came from games known as Multi-User Dungeons (**MUDs**). A MUD was a text-based game where players could communicate and interact with other people. Being text-based meant that the focus was on the gameplay and social interactions, but there were MUDs that had graphics later in the genre's life span. For many people, MUDs were the first way to communicate and socialize with other gamers without having to be in the same room as them. When the internet started to become normalized, MUDs could be played on bulletin board systems (BBS).

Having a huge community and being able to socialize as well as compete with other people differentiated MUDs from other games at the time. These elements would become the foundation for what attracted consumers to MMOGs.

There have been many MMOGs released, which led to the crash that I'll be talking about in Section 3.1, but there are several that are considered the most

DOI: 10.1201/9781003265115-2

recognized on the market for different reasons (fig 2.1). Just like with the other genres discussed in the *Game Design Deep Dive* series, trying to figure out what was "the first" game is tricky. There is the argument that the first MMOG would be *Island of Kesmai* developed by Kesmai and first released in 1985. The game was played on the CompuServe internet platform. Other games that were considered early MMOGs were *Meridian 59* (released in 1996 by Archetype Interactive) and *The Realm Online* (first released in 1996 by Sierra Online).

When it comes to pop culture and the genre at large, there are two games that became the definitions of MMOGs. *Everquest* developed by Verant Interactive and first released in 1999 is the first 3D MMOG to become a massive success and the first real blueprint for other developers to follow with their MMOGs (fig 2.2). The game has been supported with multiple expansions over the years, with a sequel released in 2004.

With that said, the game that many people consider to be "the" MMOG would undoubtedly be *World of Warcraft* (*WoW*), released in 2004 by Blizzard Entertainment. Everything about *WoW* could easily fit a design book of its own at this point. What made *WoW* successful was iterating on the MMOG formula popularized by *Everquest* and doing everything within their power to make the game approachable to a large audience. To say that *WoW* was a hit would be an understatement, the game has earned billions in revenue and had the highest subscriber base ever of a MMOG of around 12 million at its peak.

In the next chapter, I'm going to talk about the boom and crash of the MMOG market, and *WoW* was instrumental in both. Many of the lessons and mistakes designers had to learn the hard way about the mobile and F2P markets were first

Figure 2.1

The MMOG genre when it blew up would become the start of live service design.

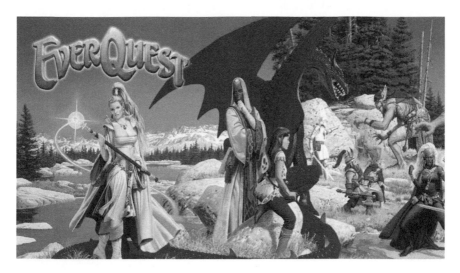

Figure 2.2

The original *Everquest* would set the stage for the MMOG genre and is still being played and updated to this day.

seen with the crash of MMOGs. With the rise of F2P and mobile games in today's market, MMOGs have lost a lot of their allure and subscriber bases, with the best-selling now peaking in the two-million player-base range.

The MMOG genre was the first example of developers working on a live service game that I'll talk about more in Section 2.4. For the industry in the 2000s, it was considered the only genre that could be viable under a live service model, but that changed with *Team Fortress 2* and *League of Legends*.

2.2 Team Fortress 2

Team Fortress 2 was first released in 2007 by Valve and was one of the games I talked about in *20 Essential Games to Study*. This would be one of the first games that wasn't a MMOG to go the live service route or "Games as a Service." The original release was a multiplayer team-based shooter, where two teams would choose to play as different classes with unique roles (fig 2.3). The game was sold as part of a compilation of Valve games known as *The Orange Box* and promoted their digital platform Steam, which would also go on to redefine the industry as we know it today.

In 2008, Valve released what would become the first of many updates to the game. The "Gold Rush Update" added in a new game mode in the form of payload, and what would become a gold mine for Valve: items. Originally, *Team Fortress 2*'s different classes were fixed in terms of their abilities and utility from match to match. Starting with this update, Valve began to add in items that would change how a class would behave. "Sidegrades," as they have become known as, are items

Figure 2.3

Team Fortress 2's style and growth of its brand and content would make it proof that live service design could be done outside of MMOGs.

or choices in a game that give the player something at the cost of something else. This allows designers to change how something works and balance it by altering another facet of that gameplay.

From there, Valve began to introduce **itemization** into the game, with all nine classes eventually getting items of their own. In 2009, the "Sniper vs Spy" update introduced another major detail of adding value to a game in the form of cosmetic items. What started as just hats for the different classes would soon spawn a litany of items that players could use to personalize their favorite classes. **Personalization** is an important aspect and major source of income for many games, something I'll be talking more about in Section 6.4.

In 2010, the next major element was added to the game in the form of an in-game store (fig 2.4). Originally, items for characters could only be unlocked by completing achievements that were introduced in updates. Later, Valve made it so that each player would get a certain number of random items while playing over a week. The final update to the system, which is still used to this day, was that the game would perform a check for a player every 25 minutes of play to decide whether to reward the player with an item. This can occur up to 10 hours of play a week. With the "Mann-conomy" update, the store allowed players to spend real money to get any specific item they wanted. The impact of this one update cannot be understated in terms of its impact on F2P design and monetization systems.

This is also when we began to see the values of time and money being represented in a F2P game – a vitally important concept of monetization that I will talk about in Section 6.5. The store would also allow **modders** to create their own items, which was added to Steam's workshop system that provides easy access

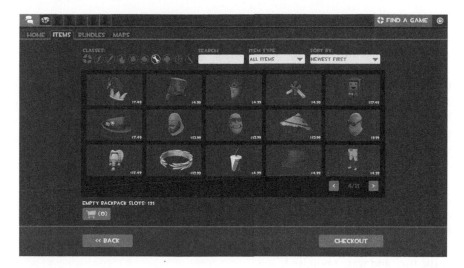

Figure 2.4

The in-game shop provides a way for people to acquire items fast, but still gives free players a chance to randomly get them through play.

to **mods** and player-created content. Items that became popular were integrated into the game, with creators receiving royalties for each purchase.

There have been many more updates to the game that have added more content and game modes, but the last update I'll talk about came in 2011 when *Team Fortress 2* officially became F2P. Transforming a game from a retail purchase to the F2P model is no small feat, something many MMOG designers had to do when the market crashed, which I'll return to in the next chapter. With *Team Fortress 2*, nothing in terms of the basic gameplay and systems was altered and it was possible to still play the game without spending money and be competitively viable.

When it comes to the success and methodology of F2P games, *Team Fortress 2* in a way became the blueprint that many games have copied. It remains one of the few games that is fair to both paying and nonpaying consumers. While it's time at the top of the genre has passed, it is still actively played by fans. With that said, the next game is still considered one of the top games in the world.

2.3 *League of Legends*

League of Legends was first released in 2009 and was built to be a spiritual successor to the game *Defense of the Ancients* or more commonly known as *DOTA*. Originally a mod for the game *Warcraft 3* (developed by Blizzard Entertainment and released in 2002), it inspired Riot Games' founders Brandon Beck and Marc Merrill to create their own version, which would turn into *League of Legends*.

Both *DOTA* and *LOL* belong to a subgenre of real-time strategy games known as "multiplayer online battle arena" (**MOBA**). A MOBA was about playing in the same viewpoint as a real-time strategy game, but instead of controlling armies or building bases, players controlled one character or "champion" and teams would fight against each other (fig 2.5). The champions themselves were all unique characters with their own abilities and roles, with team composition being a huge deal. Each champion belonged to a different role and would help the team in different ways. Mastering the gameplay required learning about the various roles but also learning different champions to best support your team's composition.

What separated *LOL* from other games starting out was that unlike *Team Fortress 2*, which was originally launched as a retail purchase, *LOL* was free to download from day one. In today's market, releasing games for free is common, but that was not the norm in 2009. Consumers could buy the game at any game store, but this was simply a way of buying access to all the champions in the game at the time and wasn't required.

Monetization was built on two aspects: buying champions and buying cosmetics. Each week the game would rotate free champions that anyone could use regardless of if they owned them or not. To permanently unlock a character, players had to spend either the free currency or its premium currency, known as Riot Points. This meant that over time someone could accumulate enough free currency to buy champions they like, or just spend the money outright on Riot Points and buy the champions quicker.

Figure 2.5

League of Legends popularized MOBA design thanks to its diverse and ever-growing pool of champions and challenging competitive play.

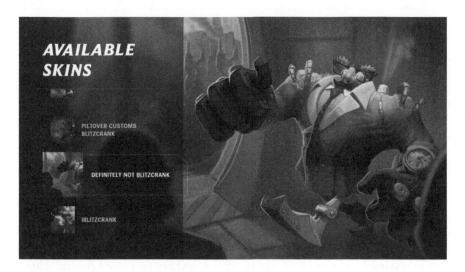

Figure 2.6

Skins, or cosmetics, that greatly change a character's original look are often sought after by people wanting to show off compared to people using the starter skins.

Cosmetics were in the form of new costumes and models for the different champions, otherwise known as "skins." Characters had different skins, ranging from changing a few details to those that completely change the look, graphics, and sound effects of that champion (fig 2.6). Players could only buy skins using Riot Points and not the free currency. The use of the different currencies and monetization models will be discussed more in Chapter 6.

The high skill curve and proficiency required to play attracted a hard-core fanbase to the game, and not requiring a price tag meant that anyone could try the game and see if they would like it. Over the years, the game and property has been expanded dramatically from its 2009 launch. There are now over 150 champions at the time of writing this book. The property itself has grown with books, music records from characters in the game, the show "Arcane," and, of course, its **Esports** impact.

League of Legends, being free to play, combined with the high **skill ceiling** made it perfect for the Esports market. Today, there are tournaments and teams all around the world, with its annual world championship being one of the most watched in Esports with a huge prize pool.

Team Fortress 2 and *League of Legends* proved that live service design could work and would become the initial template for many developers and change how games were designed.

2.4 Live Service's Impact

Live service's success with the games mentioned in this chapter, among many others, would go on to change how games were developed in the 2010s. Traditional video game development from the 1980s into the 2000s was focused on the release of a game being the end of development. With the exception of bug fixes and patches, once a game came out, that was the end of making more content for it. Games that became popular, especially multiplayer ones, would get what was called an "expansion pack," which was considered a mini sequel with new content added to the main game.

Even with expansions, video games only had so much content to keep people interested in playing. For multiplayer titles, the thrill of playing against other people was enough to keep hard-core communities alive and would be the basis for the rise in popularity of Esports and competitive play. This is also an example of **player-generated content** that I will be returning to in Section 11.2.

Live service design has fundamentally changed what consumers come to expect out of a game in today's market. If you are trying to build any large multiplayer-focused title, you are also creating a live service game, whether you want to or not (fig 2.7). The reason is that consumers want to know that the game they're playing is going to continue to receive updates and more content added (fig 2.8). The second a live service game says that there is no new content coming starts the countdown to when people are going to stop playing it and move on to another game. For multiplayer games, this can destroy any attempt at playing the game in the future if there is no community to find other people to play with. As an aside, this is also why game preservation of multiplayer titles can become trickier than single-player games if the servers that maintained the multiplayer experience have been shut off by the studio.

Figure 2.7

Live service design enabled Valve to support and grow *Team Fortress 2* beyond anything they could have done being limited to a retail purchase.

Figure 2.8

Many roguelikes have received months and sometimes years of additional support to flesh out the experience and provide more value to fans.

There is a lot that I'm going to be talking about in this book on the finer details of live service, and it has even affected single-player development. Many **AAA** games are now designed around the idea of having additional scenarios and content added as **DLC** after release. These additional purchases can push a $60 purchase to easily over a hundred dollars for a single game once all the DLC has been tallied. For games that have both single and multiplayer content, oftentimes the multiplayer components will receive more updates while leaving the single-player side alone, like with the *Call of Duty* franchise. With that said, single-player games that are given additional months or years of support can reach a point where the developer says "enough" and considers the game to be fully finished in terms of content.

Live service design is one of the most lucrative and riskiest genres to develop - a game for– something I will go into more detail about in Section 4.6. There are a lot of lessons that developers don't learn about the F2P market until it is too late, and some of them came out of what I'm going to talk about next.

3

The Beginning of the Free-to-Play Era

3.1 The MMOG Boom and Crash

Following the mega success of *World of Warcraft* in 2004, the game industry entered a MMOG boom period. The market for MMOGs was global, with major publishers like Nexon that capitalized on publishing games from countries such as Japan and Korea. NCSoft published many MMOGs in both the Eastern and Western markets, including *City of Heroes* by Cryptic Studios in 2004 and *Guild Wars* by Arena.net in 2005. This was also the period of blockbuster franchises that would go on to become fixtures in pop culture, and there were MMOGs based off *Star Wars*, *The Lord of the Rings*, *The Matrix*, and many more (fig 3.1).

During this decade, major game companies and publishers began looking for their own MMOG to stake their claim on the market despite not having prior experience, with EA publishing Westwood Studios' *Earth and Beyond* in 2002 and Square Enix releasing *Final Fantasy 11* in 2002. By the end of the decade, there were several dozen MMOGs, all released and trying to stay afloat.

Despite the success of *WoW*, it did not leave a healthy MMOG market. Other developers were either trying to make the next "*WoW* killer" or a game that would at least manage even a quarter of what *WoW* was bringing in. The problem

DOI: 10.1201/9781003265115-3

Figure 3.1

Another allure of playing MMOGs from established franchises was being able to inhabit that world and see new experiences unique to the game.

was very simple: not one game ever managed to come close to *WoW* at its peak. A major point about live service games that I'm going to return to throughout this book is the fandom and cultural impact the biggest names have. There is a difference between someone who is a fan of a certain game or brand and someone who is a fan of the genre.

Every competitor to *WoW* thought that the MMOG market was at least ten million consumers, as that was what *WoW* was averaging during its heyday. That wasn't the case: *WoW* as a property had a fandom at that level, and those people were not going to be switching to another game. In Section 11.1, I'm going to talk about why retention is one of the most important attributes of the success of a live service game. With *WoW* being both the biggest and highest rated MMOG, consumers weren't interested in trying a game like *WoW* or one that their friends weren't playing. What ended up happening was that the rest of the MMOG market was left fighting over a far smaller consumer base of people who were interested in MMOGs, but not in *WoW*'s design (fig 3.2).

Compounding issues for developers was the investment of trying to play these games in the first place. During this period, every MMOG required not only the initial purchase, but also a monthly subscription fee; with the average being between $10 and $15 a month. One of the reasons for the move to F2P by the industry was removing that initial price barrier that kept people from trying out games in the first place. The cost of developing a MMOG, especially one that could try to compete with *WoW*, was on the higher side of development costs for the time. Then there were the operating costs of not only maintaining a staff to keep working on content but also people to troubleshoot issues in the game,

Figure 3.2

What kept smaller games like *Guild Wars* from going under was appealing to the demographic of players not interested in *WoW*, and not relying on subscriptions, but expansion packs to bring in revenue.

and making sure that the servers stayed online. These additional operating costs could easily eat into any profit made by smaller MMOGs and become money sinks for the companies involved.

For the many imitators of *WoW* or those hoping for similar numbers, and there were quite a lot, they did not last. The MMOGs that survived this period did something different. Smaller MMOGs like *Guild Wars* and *City of Heroes* played differently compared to the slower pace of *WoW*. Several MMOGs during this period would go on to carve out their own specific niches of gameplay. *Second Life* by Linden Lab released in 2003 was more about living and creating in a virtual world and was one of the first MMOGs to allow people to transfer money in and outside of the game. *EVE Online* released in 2003 by CCP Games is still going strong thanks to its focus on not only ship-based combat and exploration but a persistent universe and economy.

To try and separate themselves from the other MMOGs on the market, many of the smaller and mid-tier MMOGs eventually went F2P, such as *Dungeons & Dragons Online* (released in 2006) and *Lord of the Rings Online* (released in 2007, both by Turbine Inc). What's important to remember is that these games were not originally designed around the F2P model and had to be altered in terms of gameplay and monetization. I'll go into more detail about the basic F2P elements and design in Chapter 4. Publishers such as Sony also tried to consolidate their subscriptions between games: meaning that someone could subscribe to one game and that would pay for access to all the MMOGs from the specific publisher.

What was once the dominating genre for publishers in the 2000s, MMOGs aren't as big these days thanks to the rise of mobile games and live service being adopted by the industry. The top games in the space are still earning a lot of money, but it is a far cry from the boom period.

3.2 The Rise of the Browser and Casual Game Market

While the MMOG market was going through its upheaval, new technologies and services would change the world and the game industry forever. In 2004, Facebook was first launched but did not explode in popularity until 2008. The social networking platform itself is way too big to talk about in this book. With cable modems and internet being adopted by more consumers, another option for gamers and nongamers was browser games. Browser games were typically aimed at the growing "casual market" – people who didn't normally play video games and were looking for lighter forms of entertainment. One of the most played examples of a casual game would be *The Sims*, first released in 2000 by Maxis (fig 3.3).

The industry began to see smaller studios pop up that would go to sites like Shockwave and Kongregate and would host submitted browser games as a way of starting their careers. Like the Steam digital platform, browser games didn't have to worry about having a physical store presence, and varieties of games were uploaded. This was the period where the programming language "Flash" was at its peak, with it being removed from sites and platforms in 2021. What attracted people to browser games was the fact that they were engaging enough to hold your attention for a few minutes but could be left alone and checked on at their leisure.

Figure 3.3

The Sims as a franchise would become one of the best-selling examples of casual games thanks to its wide appeal and easy to follow gameplay.

During the early 2000s, phone technology was still very limited, and attempts at making a phone that could double as a game platform failed. The technology wasn't there yet, and Nintendo was dominating the space with their handheld offerings of the Game Boy Advance and Nintendo DS. In 2007, that changed when Apple released the first iPhone and created the smartphone market. Suddenly, there were phones that were more powerful than older computers, with far more functionality than any phone that came before it. The convenience of having this device wherever people went would create the perfect platform for casual games and give the industry the first generation of mobile games that I'll talk about in Chapter 5.

3.3 The Era of Browser Game Design

Browser design still has a niche following and was the blueprint for the first generation of mobile games. Due to the game itself running off a web browser, this limits the types of games that could be produced.

For smaller browser games, they could be played in real time and were often arcade-styled games. The more popular example of browser games was the online ones, where players could communicate and interact with one another. For these games, the player must log into the game's server to issue commands or make choices that would be sent to the server, updated there, and then sent back to the user's browser with the choices made. Many browser games would focus on management or **RPG** gameplay that could be designed for an almost never-ending amount of scaling to keep people engaged (fig 3.4).

Figure 3.4

Games like *Farmville* succeeded thanks to being playable everywhere and would be the basis of monetization design for many first-generation mobile games.

To avoid competing with MMOGs, browser games were always F2P and earned their money by having a variety of smaller purchases or **microtransactions** that I will go into detail about in the next chapter. Browser games would also go on to be popularized, having 24 hour timers that dictated gameplay. Normally, in video games, time is abstracted to keep the player engaged with the **core gameplay loop**. For browser games and then later mobile games, developers would design content that would operate in real time. If the game says that something will take five hours to complete, the consumer will have to wait five hours before they can move on. A popular microtransaction is offering a way of reducing the amount of time someone must wait.

Another aspect that would be seen with browser games and then refined in the mobile space is the concept of "pay or wait." To limit how much someone can play each day, there was always a resource that dictated what someone could do, with the standard term being "energy." Every task that someone could do had an energy cost associated to it, when the player ran out, they were not allowed to do anything else until they got more energy. Energy would restore itself slowly, but another popular microtransaction was buying more energy to keep playing.

Here are three examples of browser games that became famous for different reasons. In 2003, *Kingdom of Loathing* was released by Asymmetric. The game is about a fantasy world where everything is drawn as stick figures and basic art with players creating their character from various classes. What helped *KOL* stand apart was the dry humor and the depth of its **systems**. By playing and completing quests, players would unlock more things to do, new gear, and would see more of the world. Players could spend real money to acquire unique characters and advantages, but it was possible to play the game without needing to spend money.

In 2009, the game *Evony* was released by the studio called Evony. Unlike the other games mentioned throughout this book, *Evony* is more known infamously rather than for its design. This was the first browser game to bombard websites and consumers with ads of risqué women and it wasn't possible to visit a video game site during this period without getting one of their ads. Despite that, the game itself was a strategy title and the ads did not actually reflect what was going on in the game. In a way, it did inspire false advertising that many mobile games would use to show graphics and gameplay that had nothing to do with the game in question.

Also in 2009, the game *Farmville* by Zynga was released. *Farmville* became one of the most famous casual games and turned Zynga into a household name for the mobile and browser markets. *Farmville* itself was a casual farming game where players would create farms and would unlock more items and features overtime. The game itself became synonymous with browser and casual games, and at the same time would help grow Facebook's reach.

In terms of the first generation of mobile design, *Farmville*'s gameplay and aiming for a casual audience would be reused by many mobile designers during the 2010s. In a brilliant move, *Farmville* gave Facebook users the ability to connect with one another and earn bonuses for getting their friends to play or do things on their farm, another tactic that would be copied for years. Players could spend money to acquire "gems," which was *Farmville's* **premium currency** and could be used to make the game easier, unlock higher quality goods, and more. One downside to *Farmville's* success was by becoming the standard for browser and early mobile games, it would dissuade many traditional gamers from trying mobile games and led to them ignoring mobile games for years (fig 3.5). It wasn't until the second and third generations of mobile design that consumers began to see a new focus from mobile games.

Browser games are still being played today but are held back by the limitations of browsers, while mobile technology has only gotten more powerful over the 2010s. They still retain their fans by being one of the easiest ways to play a game if you have internet access and can be quickly turned on or off at the player's leisure. There is a fanbase for being able to play board games or games with friends. **Streamers** on YouTube and Twitch will often play browser games with their fans thanks to having no barrier of entry and being able to enjoy a low-stakes game.

A popular division from browser games has been the Idle genre, made famous by *Cow Clicker* released in 2010 by Ian Bogost. Idle games are about making simple decisions and then letting the game make progress on its own, while the player does something else with periodic checks. Despite the simple origins, the genre has evolved with a lot of games, and while a fascinating genre of game design, it is not the subject of this book.

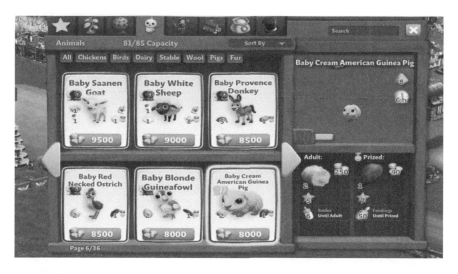

Figure 3.5

Farmville's monetization targeted people who wanted to access unique gameplay content and to improve their progress at the game.

Finally, for something higher stakes, there has been strategy-style browser games as well as on mobile. These games are all about building a base or city with armies and sending them out to conquer other player's territories. Players could group up into **guilds** or alliances to see who could become the #1 guild on a server. The general gameplay involved logging on to the game and issuing orders for your city and armies that would be carried out in real time. Players could receive alerts from the game to let them know that they are under attack, forcing someone to log on to try and counter or defend their property. While it wasn't possible to completely remove someone from the game, someone could be attacked so much that there was no way for them to recover and mount a counter-attack against the opposing player or guild. This kind of competitive **PvP** would become the basis for the second generation of mobile games that I'll discuss in Chapter 7.

4

The Basics of Free-to-Play Design

4.1 The Difficulty of Defining the Market

There is an important reason why this chapter is called "The Basics of Free-to-Play Design." The evolution of F2P design over the 2010s has led to an entirely different market and methodology for creating F2P games. There is no way that a book can tell you exactly what the future trends and designs are for the F2P genre, as every new game that becomes a success will tilt the market in a new direction (fig 4.1). In 2020, during the peak of the COVID-19 pandemic, many people found mobile and F2P games for the first time, and the market experienced a growth. At the time of writing this book at the end of 2021, the market has yet to fully see the impact of the success of live service games like *Among Us* (first released in 2018 and becoming huge in 2020 by Innersloth) and the mobile game *Genshin Impact* (released in 2020 by miHoYo).

Like the horror genre that I covered in *Game Design Deep Dive: Horror*, F2P is more of a thematic genre rather than being mechanic-based. Throughout this book, I'm going to cover the three different generations of mobile game design that evolved over the 2010s, and even with that evolution hasn't stopped developers from releasing games based on earlier generations of design. With that said,

DOI: 10.1201/9781003265115-4

Figure 4.1

Free-to-play design has grown in leaps and bounds in the 2010s, with modern examples boosting unique game systems along with monetization.

understanding what consumers have come to expect out of their F2P games is important, and I will be explaining the major trends and game systems that have defined F2P design up until this point. If at some point in the future this book gets a second edition, these chapters will have to be expanded to cover whatever new designs that have been created for the market.

4.2 The Basic Structure

Unlike some of the later concepts that I will discuss in this book, it is very easy to define what a F2P game is. A F2P game is any title that does not require an initial purchase to start playing. All you need is to install the game and it is playable immediately. By not having that initial paywall, F2P games are very easy to start playing and see whether someone is interested in playing more. The pacing of a F2P game is very important, as all F2P games are built around three distinct phases that I will go into detail about in Section 5.4.

Back in Chapter 2, I talked about live service games, and while every F2P game is a live service one, not every live service game is F2P. With that said, both will often feature the same basic elements and monetization strategies.

I will be discussing monetization in detail in Chapter 6, but to explain it briefly here, F2P games are designed to earn their revenue through microtransactions. These microtransactions could add new content, make the game easier, and unlock new features or any other service the developers can think of. A term that many mobile and F2P designers have adopted from the gambling industry is a "**whale**" to describe someone who spends a lot of money in a F2P game. For whales, they could easily spend hundreds, and even thousands, of dollars on a F2P game. Trying to attract whales, or lean into the same psychological manipulation that leads to gambling addiction, has become frown upon by the industry at large. However, it has not stopped developers from purposely designing their games in this way.

To track the player's progression, F2P games will have an account level that determines what content they have available, as well as what phase of the game someone is on. The reason why this is important is that F2P games are not designed around an end – the player is not supposed to reach a point where there is nothing left to do, and they stop playing. Instead, F2P games define what is known as "the daily loop" or what content the player is encouraged to do daily/weekly to earn rewards (fig 4.2). The purpose is to make a F2P game someone's daily activity: that they want to log in and play every day. Therefore, retention is such an important goal for F2P games; it will be discussed in Section 11.1.

Besides having an account level, progression is also defined by what kind of content the player currently has. Being able to acquire rare and powerful unlocks became the basis for **loot box** and **gacha** design that will be discussed in Chapter 6. This can also extend to cosmetic items that allow someone to personalize a character. The different monetization options will be discussed at length in Section 6.4.

An important aspect to understand about F2P games is that they are often built around very simple gameplay loops – maybe five to ten minutes of actual play at a time. The goal of the designer is to come up with gameplay that is engaging around short bursts of play that can be extended via the other game systems (fig 4.3). Often, the actual gameplay itself is not where the monetization is

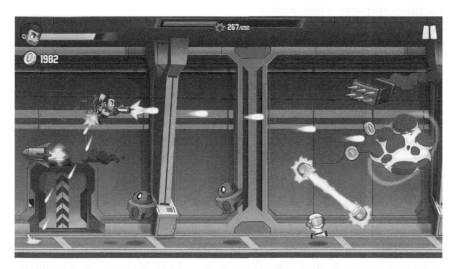

Figure 4.2

Good mobile design is all about an engaging gameplay loop that can be enjoyed for a few minutes or hours of playtime and can be played daily.

Figure 4.3

Many mobile/F2P games hook people at the start by letting them start off with powerhouse characters for the opening, and then taking them away and locking them behind a gacha or progression, such as Captain America here.

focused on, but those systems that will enhance and affect the gameplay loop. This also helps when it comes to having a quick engagement – so that someone can play a F2P game on mobile on the go, to kill a few minutes at a time, or for a lengthier experience if they want it.

4.3 Popular Genres

When it comes to the popular genres in the F2P space, this has changed based on the different generations of mobile games as well as the growth of technology in the mobile space. For the PC and major platforms, the F2P market has stayed stable to some extent, and I will start with it first.

While there are casual fans that aren't on mobile devices, the PC and major platforms are more about extended experiences as opposed to the quicker loops of mobile. Competitive games have become a popular F2P and live service option. The beauty of competitive titles is that the player base is more focused on fighting and competing as opposed to needing a constant amount of new content. In the previous chapter, I mentioned the idle genre and despite its simplicity, it has managed to hook players who will leave these games on for hours on end to make progress. For competitive titles, a single match can last anywhere from five minutes to an hour or more depending on the game in question. There are many examples of F2P games on the PC and console that are deep experiences or set up for Esports play. With no initial cost, it makes it more likely that someone will at least try the game, whereas that initial purchase may put them off.

Even though the MMOG genre is not as popular today, the MMOGs that survived the crash discussed in Chapter 3 are still around and providing different gameplay. One of the more successful examples despite a rocky start was *Final Fantasy 14* (first released in 2010 by Square Enix). The original version was met with criticism over the gameplay and general functionality that led to the studio shutting it down. When it was rereleased as *Final Fantasy 14: A Realm Reborn* in 2013, the game was noticeably better and is still one of the most popular MMOGs played at this time.

On the mobile side, genres that aren't reflex-based are popular due to the limited control functionality of a touch screen (fig 4.4). The casual market continues to bring in big numbers with all variety of puzzle games, light management games, city builders, idle games, and simple arcade titles that dominated the first generation of mobile. Games whose progression is stage-based are very popular for mobile, as it provides a very straightforward framework in terms of how to pace the player's progress and the overall difficulty of the experience. As the market entered the second and third generations, more advanced titles that focused more on competitive play and deeper systems started to appear.

Regardless of the platform, F2P games often have a heavy focus on RPG elements and abstracted design. The reason is that every player has a limit on how far they can play skill-wise, but in-game progression can be extended indefinitely. This is also why turn-based combat is so popular, as it's not reflex heavy, and it is more about out planning your opponent. With that said, balancing the design is a tricky aspect of F2P games built on RPG progression and I'll discuss

Figure 4.4

Games with RPG systems offer a lot of flexibility in terms of designing content and creating new characters that allow them to be extended easily compared to reflex-based games.

this more in Section 11.3. To that end, **CCGs** such as *Hearthstone* (released by Blizzard Entertainment in 2014) are popular across platforms. The pick-up-and-play nature of them has made them very popular on mobile devices, and there are no reflex skills required to play them.

Due to the touch screen, and the way it emulates the functionality of a mouse pointer, strategy games and their subgenres are also popular on mobile devices. While they often lack the depth of older examples, streamlined examples can still be played on mobile devices. The tower-defense genre that originally started as a mod for *Warcraft 3* has seen countless examples and has evolved with the integration of gacha design.

For action-focused or reflex-based gameplay, these games are popular on PC and major platforms, but that hasn't stopped them from appearing on mobiles (fig 4.5). For mobile action games, the **UI** must be designed not only for the touch screen, but it must be comfortable to play while holding the phone at the same time. There are also peripherals sold for mobile phones to provide basic gamepad functionality to the device. Another popular genre that has seen many examples is the "idle MMOG." In these games, the player's focus is on equipping their characters and issuing basic commands while their characters move automatically to complete quests and fight enemies.

What's important to remember is that the popularity of the genres also ebbed and flowed as monetization practices changed over the decade. The tactics that popularized the first- and second-generation mobile games are not seen as much today with how the market has changed. That change has led to developers

Figure 4.5

Reflex-based mobile games have become more popular over the 2010s but making sure they feel right in the player's hands compared to a gamepad can be tough.

Game Design Deep Dive

looking for new genres to build their F2P design and monetization systems off. One such example is the rise of "hero collectors," or games that are about collecting unique characters. This kind of design fits perfectly with RPG progression, can be attached to a variety of gameplay loops, and allows the use of gacha design that I'll come back to in Section 8.3.

Another genre perfectly suited to mobile that surprised people with its success was location-based games. The concept is that the game takes the GPS data of the user into account and sets up gameplay and exploration based on the user's local and regional location. *Pokémon Go* (first released in 2016 by Niantic) became a massive phenomenon when it first came out. Combining the design of catching the Pokémon with having to walk around outside made it popular among kids and parents. The augmented reality of the game showed Pokémon in the actual environment through the phone itself.

4.4 Can Any Genre Become F2P?

In the first section of this chapter, I mentioned the difficulty of providing an accurate representation of the state of the F2P and live service market. Part of that has been how developers have been trying to create new markets and the changes in design between the second- and third-generations of mobile devices.

For today's market, it's hard to find a genre that couldn't be altered around live service and F2P design. While multiplayer genres are the stronger fit, that hasn't stopped developers from building games around single player content with maybe a light multiplayer system added on. The key is in determining what the monetization and progression systems are going to be for the game. Monetization and progression go together when designing a F2P game, as there should not be a point where there is an actual end to the experience. Another detail is that the mobile market due to the sheer influx of F2P games has rejected paying a lot upfront for a video game; with games priced at $10 or more often not doing as well as their console or PC versions.

The games that have made F2P and live service design work the best are those that are scalable in terms of their content (fig 4.6). Single player, or linear games with fixed content, don't work as well when a designer tries to add F2P elements to it. The more you try to "twist" the genre to work with the F2P design, the more those systems will stick out and hurt the experience.

An example of this was *Middle Earth: Shadow of War* released in 2017 by Monolith Productions. The game gave the player the option to spend money to get resources, progress faster, and unlock better characters to help them (fig 4.7). While the developers said that these purchases were optional, the game's difficulty was intentionally designed to spike in the final chapter – requiring either far more time spent to win or spending money to get those advantages. Intentionally making the game harder or reducing the player's ability to play to get them to spend money is an easy way to get people to stop playing a game.

Figure 4.6

The best genres for F2P design must be built on long-term progression, so that the game can be continually extended.

Figure 4.7

Shadow of War having microtransactions in an already full retail game was one of the signs that developers were going too far with monetization in their games.

Thanks to so many mobile and F2P games on the market today, consumers are wiser to monetization tricks and will leave a game in droves if it appears to be exploitative. With *Shadow of War*, the blowback was so extreme that the developers were forced to remove those systems and purchases and completely rebalance the game around those changes.

In the previous section, I talked about examples of social and multiplayer games that became popular in the mobile and F2P space. The best genres to build F2P around are multiplayer-focused, as it helps to cut down on the amount of content that needs to be designed for keeping people engaged. Spending months to create a new two-hour quest gives you far less bang for your buck compared to creating new maps or characters that can be integrated into the entire multiplayer experience. However, the most successful games in this space tend to attract a wide audience and will design content to accommodate as many different play styles as they can.

4.5 The Introduction of "Fun Pain"

When the industry began to shift toward F2P and live service design, there was one question that developers were stumped by: "how do we get people to spend money?" When I discuss the second and third generations of mobiles and F2P later in this book, this question gets a different answer. Back in the late 2000s and early 2010s, the problem developers had was trying to transition retail games to the F2P model.

One of the most successful and controversial design elements created was the concept of "fun pain." This was the method of purposely introducing **pain points** and problems with the gameplay of a title and requiring the player to spend money to fix it. The idea was that someone would enjoy the game so much that they would be willing to spend money to make it better to play or reduce frustrating elements (fig 4.8).

Figure 4.8

This classic "Penny Arcade" strip talking about the game *Hellgate: London* may have been over-the-top but hit the mark of how developers often treated free players vs. premium ones.

This began a trend of looking at a title and taking as many **quality-of-life** (or QOL) features that made a game better and put a price tag on them to get consumers to spend money. An effective strategy was selling two different versions of a F2P game: the "free" version and the "premium" version. The free version would come with numerous downsides and pain points left in to make the experience worse in various aspects (fig 4.9). For RPGs, developers would typically limit how many items the player could store in their inventory or even what items they could equip in the first place. Systems that would make the game easier to play were removed from the free version and could only by accessible to those that were subscribed.

If this sounds very unethical to you, then you are correct. Purposely making your game worse for nonspending players is an example of bad game design and one of the aspects of a P2W game. Despite that, this kind of monetization practice became popular and is still used in smaller capacity to this day. Any time a game limits basic features or has something that was never a problem in a retail version of the game is an example of fun pain. Fortunately, the market has responded in the late 2010s with consumers pushing back hard against fun pain. With so many mobile and F2P games on the market today, a developer can't make their game worse and expect consumers to keep playing – they'll move on to any of the dozens or hundreds of similar games on the market.

What we see today is that instead of lowering the experience for free players, developers make a good experience better for those who pay. The adage "you can

	LEGENDARY Monthly Game Pass	PREMIUM Accumulated spending*	FREE Play For Free!
	Access the game, plus DLC Expansion Packs. Maximum game features unlocked!	Access the entire game and earn bonus features.	Access the entire game for free!
Game Updates	Free	Free	Free
DLC Expansion Packs	Free access **	Purchase Optional	Purchase Optional
Monthly Replay Badge Grant	150 (can purchase more)	None	None
Promethium Lockboxes	Unlimited unlocks	Keys for purchase	Keys for purchase
Character Slots	16 (can purchase more)	6 (can purchase more)	2 (can purchase more)
Inventory Slots	63 (can purchase more)	42 (can purchase more)	28 (can purchase more)
Auction Slots	20 (can purchase more)	5 (can purchase more)	0 (can purchase more)
Bank Slots	48 (can purchase more)	24 (can purchase more)	12 (can purchase more)
Trading	Items and cash	Items only	None
In-game Currency	Unlimited	2000 Max	1500 max
Chat	Unlimited	6 text chat messages per 30 seconds	6 text chat messages per 30 seconds
Send Mail	Text, items and cash	Text and items	Text only
Vault Access	Free Access Once Per Day	Free Access Every Three Days	Free Access One Per Week
Players Leagues	Can form or join	Can join	Can join

Figure 4.9

This was originally the different subscription tiers for *DC Universe Online* that it used, and how spending money offered a better experience. Since then, they have become a part of Sony's all-in-one subscription service for all of Sony's published MMOGs as part of their "Daybreak All Access" plan.

catch more flies with honey than with vinegar" applies here. I will discuss these strategies more in Chapter 6. If the experience is good and the player is happy with the game, the developer is banking on them to spend money to either make the game even better or as a way of supporting a game they love.

4.6 Creating a Live Service Game

In Section 2.4, I had begun to talk about the impact of live service design on the game industry, but now it's time to talk more about what makes a game live service. In that section I brought up how single-player games today are being released with plans for additional support in the form of DLC. While continued support is an element of live service design, those games would not be included in the agreed upon version of live service.

A live service game is one where the intent is to keep producing content for as long as the game remains profitable, and people continue to play it. Therefore, multiplayer-focused games are popular for live service, as it is easier to keep creating new content used for multiplayer than it is in a single-player experience. The goal is to find systems or content that can be expanded indefinitely – new characters, maps, equipment, cosmetics, challenges, and more (fig 4.10). For live service games that go beyond a year in terms of content, they may create new systems to help expand the game and provide more options for monetization and expansion in the future. In Section 10.3, I will be talking about two of the most popular examples of this.

Figure 4.10

A live service game will continue to be supported for as long as a game remains profitable. With *Dead by Daylight*, the developers have cornered the market on this style of gameplay since its release.

Unlike traditional games that are expanded with sequels, live service games rarely get sequels and just stick to expanding the one game for several important reasons. A developer of a live service game does not want to segment the fanbase with having two or more different games available at the same time. Second, trying to build a brand-new game and bring over all the purchases and content in the original can be very costly, or downright impossible depending on design changes in the new game. And if the developer doesn't bring something over that someone paid for, those consumers will feel cheated out of their money and most likely will never spend anything again in that game.

The only time when a sequel can be justified to consumers is when the developer can make a brand-new game with elements that couldn't fit or won't work with the previous entry. The game *Payday 2*, released in 2013 by Overkill Software, has been getting updates and new content for nine years at the time of writing this book, after only promising about three years of content (fig 4.11). While the game is still being supported, Overkill has confirmed that they are working on a sequel now, but there has not been any public information released at this time regarding what will be new in the third game.

The other aspect of creating a live service game that is important to figure out is what will be the monetization model. The earlier into development that a designer can figure this out, the easier it will be to integrate that into the gameplay and balance the design around it. No matter what, if you have any intention to continue developing a game with live service, *your game must have a monetization system in place.* Your game's monetization will fund the development of

Figure 4.11

Payday 2's gameplay has grown so much since its release and shows what "games as a service" can mean for a title. However, its continued support is not the same as the live service games seen on mobile.

new content, which will hopefully retain players and bring in new ones. Instead of someone only spending money for the initial purchase, monetization systems create the opportunity to get money from every player with each new piece of monetized content added.

What you want to avoid is adding in new monetization elements and systems after a game is out, especially if it clashes with something that was previously free or was promised not to be added. Returning to *Payday 2*, the developers caused major backlash that threatened the game's livelihood when they introduced loot box elements that they originally said would never be in the game. The push back was so strong that the developers had to remove the paying element from this system or risk a complete revolt by their community. It is okay to add new content to already established monetization systems but creating a brand-new system and charging someone for it can be seen as a cash grab if not handled right.

Another detail of live service design is the very fact that these games change over time. A live service game can be a fundamentally different experience at six months, one year, five years compared to what it was at launch. Besides adding in new content, it is not unusual to see developers improving the base experience or updating the UI with new features over time. This also requires a very careful eye toward balance and what your consumers want. Releasing an update that changes content or makes it worse for your player base can lead to most of them quitting out of frustration.

Making a live service game requires a lot of work and commitment to a project and has an enormous amount of risk to it.

4.7 The Risks and Rewards of Live Service Design

One of the reasons for the growth of live service games in the 2010s has to do with the major rewards that can come with a successful title. Game development is inherently risky; with many developers releasing their game with no idea what the market will think. This is one of the reasons why major studios like to work on sequels, as they already have an idea of what the potential fanbase will be for that title. With a live service game, the developer can continue supporting one game without the worry of making a sequel or moving on to another game. For many live service titles, as the developers get more confident in terms of support and new content, it affords them the opportunity to get creative and grow the game in new and exciting ways (fig 4.12). As I mentioned in the previous section, there are many F2P games that are fundamentally a different and bigger game than they were at their original launch.

From a community standpoint, it is far easier to build a consumer base around a game that has no barrier of entry vs. one that people must buy to play. Many retail games have free weekend events that let anyone download and play the game for a limited time, and this also has the impact of massively driving up the number of active players for that time. If a game is built around multiplayer

Figure 4.12

When a live service game does succeed, such as *Genshin Impact*, it can easily secure a company's future for years to come. Even with its first banner here, the game already proved to be a financial success.

design, going F2P and the influx of new players can be the shot in the arm to give the game a renewed chance on the market.

For the games that do blow up and become successes, live service becomes a metaphorical license to print money depending on their monetization. With *Genshin Impact*, the game made back its entire development cost within two weeks after launch and an estimated one billion in revenue for its first year.[1] When games become that big, something happens to the title in the public eye – it becomes a part of pop culture, growing even bigger and dominating the market. I will talk more about examples and how this works in Section 11.4.

One of the most important advantages is that the biggest games in the live service space become genres unto themselves and have been known to just dominate that specific gameplay. Returning to the MMOG crash in Section 3.1, everyone tried to compete with *WoW*, but no one ever managed to come close during the peak of the MMOG genre. In a way, a successful live service game becomes too big to fail, and the only things that can stop them is either a major gaffe by the studio or the developers reaching a point when it's time to move on.

With all that said, there are huge risks associated to live service games. For every live service game that becomes big, there are countless others that tried, failed, and no longer exist anywhere. Building a successful live service game goes beyond just the gameplay – you need to have a monetization model that works for you while still being fair to consumers. There must be a healthy community in place *day one* of your release to drive interest. And of course, there must not only be enough content available to keep people interested, but a roadmap of content for months or even years of support.

Consumers can smell "blood in the water," in a manner of speaking, and if a game doesn't appear to be growing, not enough people actively playing, or it's simply not good at launch, they're going to leave and never come back. This was the problem that faced the game *Evolve*'s first released in 2015 by Turtle Rock Games. Their plan was to create a 4 vs. 1 multiplayer experience with new characters and cosmetics driving the monetization. Unfortunately, consumers didn't enjoy playing the original version or the monetization model used and left the game with a community too small to support their multiplayer and continued development.

When they tried to fix things with going completely F2P in 2016, it was not enough to bring consumers back and the game closed later that year. It is very rare for a live service game to bounce back after a failed launch, with the only example that I can personally think of being *Final Fantasy 14* (fig 4.13). One other game that came close was *Star Wars Galaxies*, which was released in 2003 and developed by Sony Online Entertainment. It lasted eight years and a redesign of the gameplay was in place before being shut down.

More often, live service games are an example of "success breeding success," and having a successful launch leading to more notoriety and success over time. For many of the live service mobile games, a success for them is still earning money and growing after being out for one year.

Figure 4.13

To give credit where it's due, *Final Fantasy 14* went from being poorly received to being revived to now being considered the most-played MMOG at the time of writing this book.

Because a lot of live service games are driven by multiplayer gameplay, when/if they fail, they become unplayable and disappear from the industry. If the player is too small at launch, this can lead to a downward spiral of people trying the game, not able to find people to play with, and then leaving the game to never return.

A few paragraphs up, I said that the most successful live service games become too big to fail, and that also creates a huge risk factor for developers trying to break in. Some live service games become so big and popular that they turn into the defining game of that genre, and more importantly, they become the game that any competitors are going to be judged against. When you are trying to compete with another live service game's design, you are not competing with that game when it was released, you are going to be judged against its latest version with months/years of additional support and content. Many of the biggest successes in the mobile/live service space that are mentioned in this book have no serious direct competition, and the reason is that few have dared to try and beat them at their own game. The ones that have tried, never managed to make a real dent in the market.

There are two reasons why. The first is that any game that manages to become the defining game of a genre or style of game becomes the official standard of that design. As the standard, that game gains a huge amount of notoriety and blows up across the market, with everyone else chasing second place. Even if another game is inherently better or different compared to the standard, it will oftentimes never manage to have the same pull compared to the first hit. An example of this is with the game *Slay the Spire* developed by Mega Crit Games released in 2017 that would become the standard of the deck building roguelike genre that I talked about in *Game Design Deep Dive: Roguelikes*. Since its release, there have been many games that have all done something differently, and in some cases better than *Slay the Spire*; not one of them has gotten close to the reception and sales of *Slay the Spire* (fig 4.14).

The second reason has to do with the concepts of retention and weight that I will talk more about in Section 11.1. The longer someone plays one game, the more they become invested in it in several ways. The first one is the most obvious: money spent. If someone has played a game for several years and has spent hundreds of dollars in it, they're not going to stop one day playing the game and immediately spend that money on another game. The second investment is with the community. The social side of MMOGs carries on to a smaller extent in live service games, and why so many of them are built around joining guilds. When someone is playing with friends, they are more likely to keep playing and socializing compared to leaving the game and starting new somewhere else. It does not matter if your game is better in all respects if someone refuses to leave their guildmates and friends they made.

With all those points made, it's vital to have a healthy and growing consumer base for any successful live service game on day one. If your game is failing in any aspect upon release, the chance that you are going to be able to retain and grow that consumer base is reduced.

Figure 4.14

Slay the Spire is still the number one deck building roguelike on the market thanks to establishing itself as the first big success in that space.

Note

1. https://www.bbc.com/news/newsbeat-58707297

5

The First Generation of Mobile/F2P Design

5.1 The First Successes

Trying to put exact dates to elements or trends in the game industry is notoriously difficult as the industry moves very fast to adopt new practices and elements. With the first era of the mobile/F2P industry, I'm going to draw a line and place the first generation's start in 2007 with the release of the first iPhone. Over the next few years following the MMOG crash I discussed in Chapter 3 was when the majority of surviving MMOGs went F2P.

The very first mobile games on smartphones were either based on established franchises or were simpler games that would lead to the establishment of the casual market that I'll talk about in Section 5.3. In 2009, the industry began to see more original games being developed for mobile devices, and the first huge successes in that space would start to appear. These games managed to be the first to resonate with fans and were examples of being at the right place at the right time.

The year 2009 saw the release of what would become F2P heavyweights in the mobile space with *Farmville* and *Angry Birds* (developed by Rovio Entertainment) (fig 5.1). I already talked about *Farmville* in Section 3.3, but the game was also released on mobile to huge success. *Angry Birds* was one of the first mobile/F2P

DOI: 10.1201/9781003265115-5

Figure 5.1

The first generation of mobile, like with *Angry Birds*, catered to the growing casual game market with easy-to-pickup games that were tough to master.

games to see the explosion of success mentioned in Section 4.7. The game was about the player launching birds at fortifications set up by green pigs. To win a stage, the player had to destroy all the green pigs within a certain number of bird launches, and then they were given a rating between 1 and 3 stars based on their success.

For monetization, the developers went with having an ad-free version that players had to buy or play the game for free and get frequent ads during play. The simple gameplay and pick-up-and-play approach made it a huge success. The characters and IP of *Angry Birds* would spawn multiple spin-off games, several sequels, an animated series, and two movies at this time, and the characters were licensed off to all manner of products. The monetization Rovio used also changed in later games, adopting popular options like cosmetics and gacha systems. The first game reportedly cost only $140,000 to make, and the brand has made Rovio billions over the 2010s.

Besides puzzle and management games, simple arcade games also became huge hits for casual fans. *Fruit Ninja* was released in 2010 by Halfbrick as one of many games that were built on the competitive nature of "score chasing." The player's goal was to use the touch screen to slice fruit that would appear on the screen for points while avoiding bombs. The monetization of the game was focused on an in-game shop where the player could buy resources and other items, along with having ads. The game has since been ported to other platforms, has been downloaded millions of times, and has also earned millions in revenue. This kind of gameplay could also be seen in the hit VR game *Beat Saber* released in 2018 by Beat Games.

Halfbrick would also have another success in the market with *Jetpack Joyride* released in 2011. This was another game built on score chasing but was a part of the popular "endless runner" genre. The goal of an endless runner is to dodge objects and collect items for points (in some games) while the game gets progressively faster, with the run ending once the player runs into an object. Through play, the player could unlock items or bonuses that would make the game easier and let them get further on future runs, along with spending money on cosmetics and special advantages. The game has had millions of downloads and both it and *Fruit Ninja* have planned sequels coming at some point.

In 2011, the studio King released *Candy Crush Saga* and would become one of the biggest examples of the "Match-3" puzzle genre. The goal is to clear boards full of candy by moving them around to match three or more at one time to remove them. The match genre has been a popular one among the casual market, and even has been used as the foundation for more advanced games across the different platforms. The game earned money by allowing the player to buy premium currency that could be spent on items that would make the game easier. Since its success, King became one of the major names in the mobile space and has earned millions yearly with people still playing it at the time of writing this book.

A popular money maker on mobile and in the live service space are games with competitive elements to them, and *Clash of Clans* released in 2012 by Supercell is one of the biggest (fig 5.2). The game combined the concept of building a city with light real-time strategy of sending armies to attack enemy castles. The main

Figure 5.2

Clash of Clans is one of the biggest examples of both pay or wait monetization and the use of PvP modes to drive competition and spending.

element of its monetization was a kind of fun pain that is commonly referred to as "pay or wait." Every aspect of playing *Clash of Clans* revolves around constructing structures or raising an army using the game's two primary resources of gold and elixirs. To get more, players must build increasingly more expensive structures that also increase in the amount of time to finish constructing. Everything in the game can be sped up with spending the premium currency of gems. At the higher levels, your city will get invaded by other players and you will need to construct additional defenses and military units to fight them. Having players compete to have the best clans would drive purchases of gems and make it one of the most lucrative games of its kind, earning over an estimated 400 million with in-game purchases.

The Match-3 formula has seen many different takes on it, and *Puzzle and Dragons* by Gungho Online (released in 2012) is one of the biggest. Combining Match-3 gameplay with gacha design, the game is far more complicated than *Candy Crush Saga*. Players build teams of monsters to go on quests and grow in power. Every monster belongs to a different element and has different powers the player can use in battle. When the player makes a match, the monsters of that specific elemental color will attack the enemies. Special powers can do everything from helping the party to influencing the board itself. Acquiring new monsters requires the player to find eggs to hatch monsters of different rarities. Looking back at the market, this is one of the earliest examples of gacha and mobile design combining that would become huge throughout the 2010s. To this day, the game remains one of the best-selling mobile games in Japan and has earned over seven billion dollars over the decade, and even had a collaboration spin-off game with Nintendo.

This era of mobile and F2P games seemed to be dominated by whatever was "the next big thing," and one of the most surprising successes was *Flappy Bird* developed by Dong Nguyen and released in 2013. The game's simple premise was tapping the screen to cause your bird to flap with the goal to fly between pipes for as long as you can. The simplistic gameplay attracted people to keep playing to see how far they got. Instead of in-game purchases, the game featured ads that would play regularly. The game became a sensation and was earning Dong $50,000 a day in ad revenue.[1] The game was met with controversy, with Dong eventually taking it offline because he felt it was hurting people with how addictive it was. Even with the game taken down, that didn't stop many imitators and **clones** being made to capitalize on the success (fig 5.3).

Besides the games listed in this section, the idle genre that I mentioned in Section 3.2 also took off on mobile, with far too many to try and list here. The combination of the portability of smartphones paired well with the hands-off nature of idle games. Many popular idle games that were available on the PC also had mobile versions, with both usually sharing the same monetization systems. *Cookie Clicker* by Julien Thiennot may have been released after *Cow Clicker* in 2013, but it has become one of the most successful and recognizable idle games. Later idle games would add more strategy beyond just idling, with two great

Figure 5.3

The problem with many first-generation mobile games is that their simplistic game-play made them very easy to be copied by other studios, leading to a pattern of clones appearing for every popular game.

examples being *Clicker Heroes*, released in 2014 by Playsaurus, and *Realm Clicker*, by Divine Games released in 2015.

For all the mobile games that are going to be discussed in this book, there are ways of playing them without needing a smartphone. Some have been ported to other platforms, but many people use software on the computer to emulate a smartphone and play the games there. At this time, the most popular example is using the software "Bluestacks," but not every mobile game can be played that way and some companies don't like people playing their game this way.

This era of mobile and F2P games proved two things to the industry: that there was huge money in mobile games, and there was officially a casual market.

5.2 Cultivating the Casual Market

A major shift in the consumption of video games happened with the rise of mobile and F2P games. The industry in the 2000s made great strides to become farther reaching and more approachable outside of the hardcore market. With the rise of the mobile market, publishers and developers would come to embrace casual gamers.

Despite the popularity of it in mobile, there has been a market for casual games before it. During the 2000s, two of the biggest names in casual games were Popcap Games, who released hits like *Peggle* and *Plants vs. Zombies* in 2007 and 2009, respectively, and Big Fish Games, who became both a developer and a place to find all varieties of casual games (fig 5.4). One of the most popular casual games was *The Sims* and has often been credited as one the first casual games.

Figure 5.4

With *Plants vs. Zombies*, Popcap Games created an amazing game for casual and hardcore fans of tower defense gameplay, while streamlining as many complexities as possible out of the design.

The casual game market is defined by games that are easy to play, often have very little to no stakes, and was aimed at audiences that weren't typically targeted by other companies. Many casual games would become popular with women and would often feature female leads. The company Artifex Mundi created a niche for itself with its "hidden object adventure games" that combined adventure game puzzle solving with hidden object gameplay.

But it wasn't until the mobile market that the greater industry began to understand that there was in fact a market for casual gamers. Unfortunately, getting accurate stats about the industry before 2010 is difficult, as there wasn't a lot of record keeping done. In 2010, the Entertainment Software Association (or ESA) began releasing annual statistics of the game industry. In the 2010 report[2] covering 2009, the ESA found that the market was split as 60% male and 40% female, with the most successful games being *Call of Duty Modern Warfare 2* and *The Sims* on console and PC, respectively. In the 2016 report that covered 2015,[3] casual games became the second best-selling genre for computer games.

In the most recent report (at the time of writing this book) for 2020,[4] more people today now play video games on their smartphones than on console and PC. In terms of gender, 55% of those that identify as male play video games and 45% identify as female, and the most preferred genre was casual games across the different age groups that were polled (fig 5.5). The games that were discussed earlier in this chapter, and the ones that are coming up, have all been incredibly popular and profitable. It has been reported that mobile games made at least

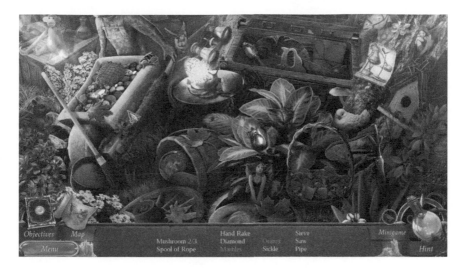

Figure 5.5

Developers like Artifex Mundi catered to women with their casual games, but one of the trends of the 2010s was about dispelling the myth that women didn't play video games.

10 billion dollars in revenue in 2020 and experts believe that the market will continue to grow with each passing year.

The boom of mobile over the 2010s saw a push by every major developer and publisher to try and capitalize with their own games; with many of them opening specific branches and studios dedicated to mobile games.

5.3 The Limits of the Casual Market

The casual market became one of the dominate strategies for developers and publishers over the 2010s, and essential for the rise of the mobile industry. However, as the decade went on, developers, both new and established, were learning a harsh truth about casual gamers (fig 5.6).

There is something I like to say a lot when talking about game design and the market as a whole: there is a difference between someone who is a fan of a genre vs. a fan of a game/IP. The industry has been built on the idea of indirect competition – that if someone is a fan of genre A, they're going to buy more than one game of said genre. Direct competition means that if someone must decide between buying item A or item B, once they make their choice, they're not going to buy the other item as well.

The misconception about the casual market is almost word-for-word the same that plagued the MMOG boom and bust that I discussed earlier. Developers assumed that when looking at a game like *Candy Crush Saga* or *Clash of Clans* that all those people who played those games would also be

Figure 5.6

Candy Crush Saga became one of the defining mobile games and King's claim to fame, but also left no room in the market for any other Match-3 games to try and even compete with them.

interested in other examples, and of course, something that could take that design further.

However, that is not the case – for the many people who became huge fans of the games mentioned in this chapter, they did not move on to other games. The casual gamer market is not made up of people who follow the industry trends and news. They're not interested in going from game-to-game or trying something new. In Section 4.7, where I laid out the risks of live service games, casual gamers are affected even more by the weight of money spent and community compared to hardcore gamers.

And just like the MMOG crash, once people found their "*World of Warcraft,*" that's it, they're not going to look for another game to play. The mobile market for the 2010s could also be defined as oases in a desert – with few games succeeding huge and the rest struggling. One of the reasons for the different generations of mobile/live service that I'm discussing in this book is that designers were trying to find new ways to entice people. They knew that they couldn't make a more profitable version of *Clash of Clans* or *Farmville*, so the question became: "what kind of gameplay has not been done yet, and is there a market for it?" (fig 5.7).

With that said, I need to point out another misconception, many gamers and people in the industry see casual gamers as "lesser" compared to people who play established genres and well-known franchises. That someone who plays *Clash of Clans* doesn't do anything special compared to a *Call of Duty* player. However, there are people who play casual games for hundreds of hours and many of the more popular mobile games even have competitive tournaments. It does take

Figure 5.7

Much of the strategies of the second and third generation of mobile is about finding new genres and designs to convert to mobile play, such as the fighting game genre.

a lot to play a mobile/live service game at the highest levels, especially if there is a competitive aspect to it. For this book, when I refer to people as "casual" or "hardcore," I'm referring to their overall skill at the game they're playing, not their entire mastery at video games. And when talking about video games directly, this will be referencing the skill level required to play them.

5.4 The Mobile Methodology

As I talked about in the previous chapter, the mobile market evolved over the 2010s, and there are going to be multiple chapters in this book dedicated to various aspects of it. Regardless of the genre and consumer base, mobile games all share similar basic qualities that I want to outline here.

The portability of smartphones and their general purpose of being used on the go is different from playing a video game on a console or computer. When someone sits down to play a traditional video game, they are setting aside time to experience the game. A single session of playing a game could be anywhere from 30 minutes to several hours depending on the game and the interest of the consumer.

With mobile games, they are designed around very quick gameplay loops, and can often average between one and five minutes of play at a time (fig 5.8). Similar in structure to roguelikes that I covered in *Game Design Deep Dive: Roguelikes*, the goal isn't to keep someone entertained for hours at a time but create an enjoyable several minutes of gameplay that can be repeated. The actual

Figure 5.8

The perfect mobile gameplay loop is something quick enough that it can be played at any time, but still have enough depth to keep someone's attention and interest in coming back. *Cookie Run: Kingdom* became big in 2021 thanks to an engaging gameplay loop that anyone can play.

play may only be five minutes long, but someone could repeat that for hours on end if they wanted to. The idea is that someone can play a mobile game anywhere and at any time but can just as quickly put it down and come back to it whenever they want.

For developers, they need to focus on a quality, but simple, gameplay loop. If it's too long, it loses the pick-up-and-play nature of mobile games; if it's too short, then there might not be enough to keep people interested in playing. Later in the book, I'm going to talk about the challenges of long-term content design for mobile games, and part of that difficulty is that it's very easy for someone to burn through content given the simple gameplay loops.

To combat this, developers will often have systems in place to either slow down their daily progress or subtly tell the player that they're finished for the day. Energy systems that were first seen in browser games have become a popular option used by many mobile games. The player can only store so much energy and will usually come back over a very slow rate. Once the player is out of energy, their only options are to either buy more, usually with premium currency, or stop playing while it refills.

The other option is to use the daily loop to focus what the player should be doing on a given day. Games will often have a quest or mission system tied to the different systems in the game. These quests can vary from playing X number of stages, using a gacha banner, play against another player, and so on. Complete

Figure 5.9

Daily and weekly tasks are always centered around the daily loop play to further incentivize doing them, and for games like *Figure Fantasy* and many others is the primary form of currency for nonpaying players.

enough quests for the day, and the player will often receive premium currency and other important resources. Once the daily reward is done, they will not earn anything extra until the next day (fig 5.9).

An advanced example of this is with the use of randomized daily quests. How this works is that the game will randomly give each player three quests to complete. These quests can be anything related to playing the game or using certain tactics to win. The harder the quest, the more the player is rewarded for doing it. The usual system is that each day the player will either get one quest or can replace one of their three quests with another randomly chosen one. The rewards from the daily quests are always far more than what someone could earn by just playing the game normally, and it makes sense from an optimization standpoint to finish the quests and then be done with the game until the next day.

The inherent goal of all mobile and F2P games is to make playing the game become someone's daily routine – something that should become a part of their schedule each day. The reason is that when a game becomes that for someone, they are more likely to keep playing, and hopefully keep paying the developer. The different ways that games try to retain players will be discussed more throughout this book, and these methodologies have changed over time.

To get someone to that point, developers need to pay attention to how playing the game changes based on where the player is at, and there are three distinct phases of this.

5.5 The Three Phases of Gameplay

Traditional video games are about having an established beginning, middle, and end to the experience. At some point, the player is going to reach the end of the game or get tired of playing, and then they will move on to the next game they want to play. With mobile and F2P games, the goal is to create an experience that someone will want to keep playing for days, weeks, months, and even years. To do that, these games are designed around a very specific form of pacing and moving the player through different phases that will hopefully hook them into continuing to play.

The first phase is the tutorial or onboarding phase. This is the period where someone is going through all the tutorials and learning every system of the game (fig 5.10). Mobile developers have learned that they want to make sure that someone understands everything there is to the game before they cut the player loose, and why tutorials in every mobile game are required to play. Developers make sure to purposely lock additional systems and UI elements that aren't needed to ensure that someone is only focusing on the task at hand. The goal is to get the player to the point of understanding all the major systems, including any tied to monetization, as quickly as possible. Often, the final tutorial is the actual monetization or gacha mechanic depending on the game. A popular design is to lock additional systems and challenges to the player's profile level, and the game will reintroduce tutorials whenever the player unlocks a new system. For rewarding

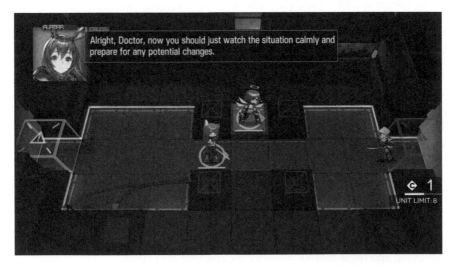

Figure 5.10

Tutorial design is an essential part of any successful game regardless of its depth. *Arknights* is one of the more complicated games and has several chapters dedicated to onboarding players about the rules and basic strategy of playing.

the player with additional resources, the onboarding phase will often grant the most as a way of enticing new players to keep at it.

The second phase is the daily loop and is about what the player is going to be doing daily. In this phase, the tutorial is done, there is no more onboarding, it is about playing the game with the training wheels off in a manner of speaking. The designer's role here is to create an engaging set of tasks that will move the player forward while keeping them entertained with the mechanics. For many F2P games, the daily loop will change based on the player's progress and what additional systems have been unlocked. Some mobile games will have more daily quests than are required to get all the goals for the day to allow the player some choice in the content that they do. Rewards will slow down somewhat, as the player should be figuring out what they need and try to get it.

The final phase is the late game play, not to be confused with the endgame of traditional games, as F2P games are not designed to end. Long-term play can mean different things depending on the game and the design in question (fig 5.11). This is where the rewards of playing are the slowest. Instead of playing trying to figure out their options, it is about finalizing and optimizing what they're using to push into the hardest content the game has to offer. The types of long-term play are divided between games that are PvP vs. those that are **PvE**.

In PvP-styled games, it becomes a contest to see who the best player is on the server, either at the individual level or in alliance vs. alliance contests. This can

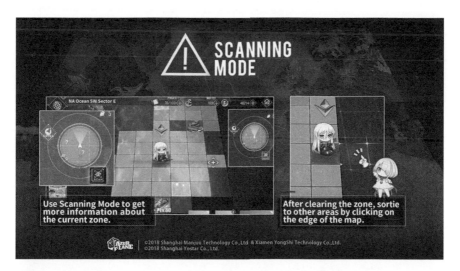

Figure 5.11

The late game content in a mobile game is often designed around new systems and/or challenges for player to complete for access to the best rewards in the game. *Azur Lane* added in the Operation Siren mode that unlocks at level 60 accounts to complete challenges for getting the materials for crafting the best gear.

lead into huge spending for players who are trying to be the best. The reason is that the top player or guild is not only rewarded with bragging rights but will be given a lot of rewards – even premium currency – for being the best. Stay at the top long enough, and someone may not need to spend real money in the game anymore as they're getting all the resources they need as the top player.

For PvE games, F2P games borrow a design from the MMOG genre with having "raid" content to challenge. Raids in MMOGs are incredibly difficult missions against enemies with their stats higher than anything else in the game previously. By beating these challenges, the player is not only rewarded bragging rights, but will often earn raid-exclusive resources and equipment that can boost their characters even higher. Story-driven F2P games will also add in new missions to extend their stories and increase the power the player needs to be to keep going.

In terms of time spent playing, as someone moves through the three loops, the amount of time someone will spend daily on the game will change. In the onboarding and daily loop phases, where rewards and progress are always coming, players will spend more time and make a lot of progress due to these bonuses. Once they have reached the late game, where rewards are more focused and rewards are lower, they may play for brief bursts of time to make as much progress they can for that day and then stop. The exceptions to this are competitive games, where the competition between players can drive the play more than earning daily resources (fig 5.12).

Figure 5.12

For games built around high-skill level play, like fighting games or *For Honor* here, playing something that offers a unique experience is often more of a draw than the rewards themselves. This is especially true for the best players who have access to everything and are only interested in competing to see who the best is.

As a designer, it is crucial to design all three phases properly, as losing the player in any of them will hurt the game's chance at surviving. Having a poor tutorial phase will leave players feeling confused and not wanting to invest more time in trying to figure the game out. A poor daily phase will bore players who don't feel like they're making noticeable progress and will quit. For the final phase, without having content for the player to aim for, they're going to stop playing, and with this group being made up of hardcore players, it is the one most likely to spend money in your game.

As an added point of challenge for developers, these three phases must be fully realized on day one if your game has any hope of retaining customers. Sometimes developers may release with just the onboarding and daily loop content done and hope to get the late game finished after launch. This can be risky, as players will quit if they find that there is nothing else in the game to hold their interest in the late game. There is a misconception among mobile developers that they will often prop up one month's revenue of a mobile game as a way of saying their game is a hit. When it comes to live service games, retention is the biggest metric for gauging the overall success. A game that has a huge first month but loses 90% of its player base the month after is most likely going to become a failed game. The three phases also represent the three different consumer bases of a game that I will go into detail about in Section 11.1.

Notes

1. https://www.polygon.com/2014/2/6/5385880/flappy-bird-collects-50k-per-day-in-ad-revenue
2. https://www.org.id.tue.nl/IFIP-TC14/documents/ESA-Essential-Facts-2010.pdf
3. https://cdn.arstechnica.net/wp-content/uploads/2017/04/esa_ef_2016.pdf
4. https://www.theesa.com/wp-content/uploads/2021/08/2021-Essential-Facts-About-the-Video-Game-Industry-1.pdf

6

The Matters of Monetization

6.1 Ad Revenue

Unlike the other genres in the *Game Design Deep Dive* series, it is important to cover monetization and the options available for F2P games. Earlier in this book I mentioned that every F2P game must have monetization to go with it, as no money means no resources to keep developing the game.

Ads were the first major monetization system used by mobile games. How this works is that the developer signs up with an ad partner. The ad partner is responsible for acquiring ads from brands and other companies that will be displayed in the game. The developer will get a programming code that will need to be placed in the game and trigger when it's time to run an ad from the ad partner. Developers will get paid based on people looking at the ad and clicking on it, with more money earned for those that click (fig 6.1).

In-game advertising can be set up to always be displayed on the UI with new ads cycled in regularly or requiring the player to view an ad to gain additional resources or to keep playing the game. Incentives for watching ads are a popular strategy to get someone to click on them without actively forcing them to. Back in Section 5.1, I mentioned *Angry Birds* and how they had an ad-filled and ad-free

DOI: 10.1201/9781003265115-6

Figure 6.1

Many mobile game companies have gotten away with misleading, and sometimes just incorrect, ads about their game to try and convince someone to play it. Many of these, such as the one for *Homescapes*, will show up in other games.

version. For games that have an ad-free version, this is oftentimes one of the most popular purchases to reduce the annoyance of ads.

While games can still be designed around ad revenue today, it has become outdated with second- and third-generation mobile games. Like fun pain, consumers don't want to be annoyed while they are playing a game anymore. If you are a developer trying to compete with a second- or third-generation game, it is not advisable to put ads in your game for today's market.

6.2 Monetization Design

The term "monetization" has become a way of describing the ways in which a game can be monetized and creating systems to facilitate that. When coming up with the monetization for any game, designers need to examine what aspects can have a price tag put on them. In Section 6.4, I will attempt to list every major example that developers have used at the time of writing this book. Monetization in F2P and mobile games is built around microtransactions, with the most popular ones designed to be "endless."

Designers know that the more someone has in a F2P game, the less likely they're going to be willing to spend. Any time a game offers the player the chance of getting something guaranteed, it is several times more expensive compared to other purchases, because this option will then cease to be worth anything once acquired. The best microtransactions from a monetization standpoint are those that the player can never have enough of (fig 6.2). In

Figure 6.2

Limited-time microtransactions are often set up to entice a player to spend money to get resources they will specifically need. Games like *Cookie Run: Kingdom* and other gacha games will often generate these sales when the player has a good pull to try and get them to spend further.

gacha-styled games, this includes the resource that is used for the gacha itself. What the player needs changes based on their overall progress in the game. It is not uncommon for resources to be weighted differently based on what the player's current objective is.

As a developer, you want to make sure that you have at least one primary monetization system – something that the player must be willing to spend real money on to acquire. You can have multiple systems, but with each system runs the risk of the player feeling like the game is trying to take advantage of them. For an example, the primary monetization in gacha games is being able to acquire more chances at the gacha to get the best rewards. It is also common to feature something of a higher quality that can only be acquired by spending money, such as premium cosmetics or skins for characters. These skins serve a dual role, they provide fans with an easy way to support the game, and it allows them to dress up their characters and look different from everyone else (fig 6.3).

When figuring out monetization, it is important to avoid having monetization tied to the core gameplay loop itself. What that means is trying to charge the player for the actual playing of the game. The reason why this is frowned upon is that by introducing microtransactions that affect play, it creates a P2W situation. During the 2010s, there were developers who tried to experiment with games where microtransactions did lead to better results during play. *World of Tanks* developed by Wargaming and released in 2010 allowed players to buy "gold," which was the premium currency. Gold could be spent on higher quality ammo

Figure 6.3

Cosmetic skins are some of the biggest money makers in mobile/F2P games thanks to being able to personalize someone's favorite character(s). *Azur Lane* focuses more on earning money through its very wide catalog of skins compared to its gacha system.

that while it cost real money to use, it did more damage and gave an advantage to paying players.

In Section 9.3, I will go more into detail about P2W and ethical design, and how you want to avoid a haves vs. have-nots situation in your game. If consumers feel that the game is only set up for people who spend money to have all the advantages, your consumer base is going to leave in droves. All monetization today is driven by a game's currency that is created for the game.

6.3 Creating Currency

Directly tied to monetization in any F2P game is the currency that the game uses. Like casinos that require people to purchase chips to play, currency in F2P games are the resources that the player must use to experience the game. The most basic example is having a "free" currency and a "premium currency." The free currency is earned by playing the game and is often tied directly to progression. Many mobile and F2P games will use the free currency as a basic universal currency for its systems, such as spending the game's version of money to acquire other general resources.

Premium currency is where most mobile and F2P games make a lot of their revenue on. This is the currency that is normally only available by spending real money in the game. For third-generation mobile and F2P games, they will often give the player small amounts of premium currency for free for making progress. Premium currency's main role is to acquire content that directly benefits the player in the game, such as new characters, exclusive features, better gear, and so on.

Both categories can be further broken down by having currency exclusive to specific systems and progression (fig 6.4). For RPGs, they may have a resource for money, a resource for experience, a resource to unlock new abilities, a resource to make gear better, and this can continue for every progression system the game has.

With premium currency, developers may take it a step further and have different kinds of premium currency that are nontransferable between them. This is often done when a game has multiple monetization systems, such as a resource for gachas and a resource for cosmetics. A newer feature seen in recent gacha games is having a double gacha resource: one is used for a general gacha, while the other is for a limited-time or "exclusive" gacha.

Multiple currencies are often used to confuse consumers on the actual monetary value and is viewed as a negative of F2P design by critics. Having just one currency that can be used for all services in the game is simpler and fairer to the consumer. Most F2P and live service games only allow for a one-way conversion of currency. There are notable exceptions such as *Eve Online* and *Second Life*. Both games allow consumers to spend real money to convert it to the respective game's premium currency, but they also allow people to convert that money back to their native currencies. Setting up this process is a very complicated matter,

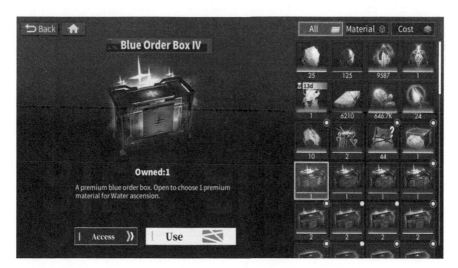

Figure 6.4

Mobile games can get quite excessive with resources and currencies, such as *Alchemy Stars* that has resources broken down into the different elemental types that must be collected.

as it requires getting approval from different countries and governments and is beyond the scope of this book.

6.4 Popular Monetization Options

There are a lot of ways that a game can be monetized, as I discussed throughout this chapter. Over the span of the 2010s, monetization has move away from the elements of fun pain and paying to make the game better, to paying money to get something that the player wants and/or supporting the developer.

The first category is about getting more resources. The most popular examples are spending money to refill the player's energy supply or acquiring more in-game money (fig 6.5). Many mobile games today will allow players to buy what's called a monthly pass, which gives them free resources every day for the month and requiring them to buy this each month. As an interesting point, mobile and F2P games have been doing more with subscription models for their games when it comes to the third generation of mobile titles; something that originally was seen as a disadvantage for MMOGs. The difference is that these subscriptions provide the player with daily resources and bonuses, as opposed to just granting access to the game.

In-game stores can also have specific bundles of similar resources that some-one can buy to get a better deal compared to buying them individually. For many F2P games, bundle offers and special sales are a great way to drive sales with a limited-time deal. It's up to the developer to figure out what resources can be

Figure 6.5

Without fail, every single mobile game will have a screen exactly like this, as a way for people with a lot of money to quickly acquire the game's premium resource. For whales in *Arknights*, I'm sure they've viewed this screen a lot.

purchased using free currency and which ones are only available with premium. Many F2P/mobile games will have seasonal sales or those for major events, where there will be deals not available at any other time. As mentioned in the previous section, if something can be unlocked permanently, it will only be available by spending premium currency.

The second category is buying methods of progressing in the game. This includes upgrade materials, gacha currency, new gear, or anything that is used to improve the player's characters. When we're talking about games built on gacha design, they may allow you to buy specific characters with certain currencies, but you won't be able to directly buy any character with premium currency. Due to the focus on RPG design, mobile games will often require the player to use different systems that each require their own resources to power up characters. A common one in gacha games is having bonuses that can be applied to a character but requiring them to use other copies of said character to unlock them (fig 6.6). Gacha design and progression based off random rewards is a huge deal that I will cover in length in Sections 8.3 and 8.4, respectively. What separates this category from simply buying power is that all the resources require the player to have characters in the first place, and those can't be bought outright.

Another category that depends on the game in question is buying services. By spending money, the player can make a certain aspect of the game easier or get more value out of their time spent playing. The use of a "battle pass" would apply here, and I will cover this system more in Section 10.4. These purchases are

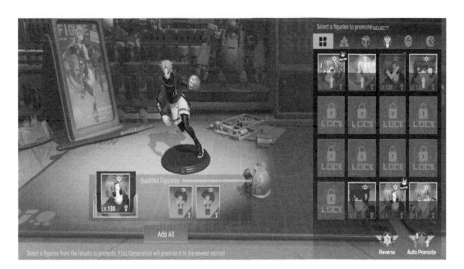

Figure 6.6

Promoting or "ascending" characters using duplicate pulls is a popular gacha trick to give someone a reason to keep spending money on a banner. With *Figure Fantasy* your entire progression is gated by your five highest characters: requiring frequent trips to the gacha.

like the monthly subscriptions of the first category, but the difference is that the player is not directly getting something by spending money here, it is rewarding the player with more for playing the game. When the time is up or the player doesn't renew it, this service and all its benefits are turned off until they spend money again.

The next category can be the most lucrative of all in a game: cosmetics. People love to personalize in video games as a way of making a character uniquely theirs or showing off to their friends and enemies. Unlike the other ones that feature game-play-affecting elements, cosmetics don't have any implications on the act of playing the game. This also means that there is no need to worry about balancing them, and a game can have as many cosmetics as their art team can keep coming up with ideas.

Cosmetics as a monetization category is only limited by the imagination of the developers. They can be as simple as changing the color palette of a character, to a skin that completely changes the look, sound effects, and graphical effects. Cosmetics can extend beyond the character and can include changing how the UI looks, any buildings the player owns, pets that can follow the player around, and many more. The more elements that the cosmetic changes will typically afford them a higher price – with some games charging upward of $30 or more for the highest quality available (fig 6.7).

This becomes even more complicated if your game has limited-time cosmetics. Every mobile and F2P game will have seasonal events for the holidays and will often have exclusive cosmetics that can only be acquired then. Some games

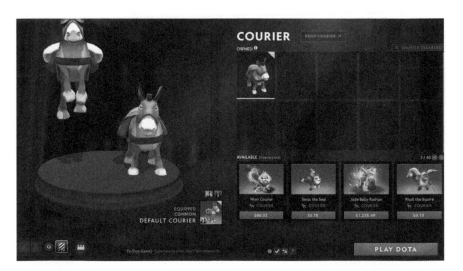

Figure 6.7

Scarcity is often one of the biggest drivers in value, and any time there is something unique, that is very limited, it will often be valued higher than anything else. Games like *DOTA 2* that allow player-to-player trading can often see a lot of money being thrown at rare items.

only have cosmetics that are available for a few months before disappearing forever – raising their value and does bring in the questions of ethics in F2P that I'll talk about in Chapter 9.

For games that allow players to buy and sell cosmetics, this creates a secondary market that can lead to lots of money being thrown around for the rarest of the rare cosmetics for that game. An early example of this was when Valve had Mac EarPods as an exclusive *Team Fortress 2* item that was only available for a limited time and for people who played the game on a Mac. After this event was over, people were spending over a 100 dollars for an item that literally did nothing in the game.

As an important aside, this has also created a black market with sites dedicated to selling these items or gambling on them outside of the rules of the game. Many sites and players of these games have been caught trying to trick people into gambling items, and this is something as a designer you need to consider if you're going to allow for the reselling of digital items.

One final point about cosmetics for this section. Cosmetics are often the one purchase in a mobile/F2P game that can never be bought with in-game currency. There have been debates about whether this would be considered ethical. I will be expanding on this in Section 9.3, but for now, having a system like this with no means of acquiring them through play is an unethical practice, gameplay affecting or not.

The goal of everything mentioned in this section is to get someone to make their first purchase in a game. That first purchase is huge for mobile developers, because it begins to give the game "weight" in the player's minds (fig 6.8).

Figure 6.8

Mobile games today all incentivize the first purchase, often having different names for it. The goal remains the same: to get someone to spend money by offering them something unique, such as *Azur Lane* offering this ship girl.

The more someone spends in a game, the less likely they're going to stop playing because of that investment. This is also referred to as the "sunk cost fallacy." I will discuss this more and how it relates to retention in Section 11.1.

To make purchases more attractive, there are ways that developers have sweetened the deal. Many will have a unique reward that can only be gotten once someone makes a purchase, no matter how much they spent. Some games will track the amount of money and will offer special rewards or more services based on the lifetime spending by the player. This practice is commonly referred to as a "VIP" system and is another way of subtly manipulating someone to spend money in a game. Unlike the other purchases mentioned, a VIP system is not tied to any one purchase, but only goes up based on the total amount of money. Having a VIP system tied only to lifetime spending is another tactic that has been frowned upon as a way of rewarding and encouraging continued paying and is akin to the use of "comps" in casinos for their biggest spenders.

Ultimately, when it comes to monetization, developers are free to explore any and every avenue open to them. Do not be afraid to try different things, as the better you can integrate the option into the game experience while still making the game enjoyable to play, the more likely people will spend on it. The advances mobile and F2P games made in terms of monetization came out of developers trying to find better and more ethical ways of presenting those options. The best F2P and mobile games will have people spend money not so much for the act of acquiring something, but to give back and support the development of the game. This is one of the hardest things to do in any title, and there are only a few examples I will talk about later in this book that have achieved that level of appreciation by their fans.

6.5 The Values of Time and Money

When it comes to putting value on any content in a video game, live service or not, it is important to understand how people value time and money differently. In this chapter, I have spoken at length about putting price tags on content in your game, but for a game to be considered "free to play," you must consider the nonpaying players.

Consumers value time and money differently based on their personalities as well as their wallets. For people who value money over time, they will do everything they can not to spend additional money in a title and are happy to make progress gradually over time. For people who value time over money, they want to experience content as fast as they can and not have to wait to access it or grind systems to be strong enough to do it (fig 6.9). If they only have a brief period each day to play a game, they want to make the most of it. For people who play games to collect characters, they want to make sure that they have access to everyone. It is not about speeding through the act of playing the game but getting to the content and experience they want as fast as possible.

Figure 6.9

Mobile developers will always provide ways of skipping any kind of grinding in their games for players who want it, as with these packages from *Cookie Run: Kingdom*. But when a game favors those who spend money too much, then it becomes a problem and a poor experience for nonpayers.

You might think that it is not important to care about nonpaying people in your game, "if they're not spending money, why should I cater to them?" The reason is that putting too much of a focus on money – trying to monetize every single aspect of the game – people are going to view the game as being P2W and the developers greedy and will not support them. However, if people who value time more do not have the means of progressing at the rate they want to, they will stop playing a game that demands more of their already limited time.

Your goal as the designer is to figure out how to cater to both groups as evenly as possible with your game's monetization system. Returning to *Team Fortress 2* from Section 2.2, Valve was one of the first developers to make a game that was fair for everyone without upsetting the balance of the game. By spending money someone could get all the hats and all the items they wanted. For a free player, they would get access to the same items over time, and while they were not in control over what they got, they were still getting rewarded for playing the game. And no matter how much someone spent in the game, it never replaced the importance of learning the classes and skill when it came to winning.

The challenge is not to restrict free players compared to paying ones, but that both groups should get to the same point in the game and be able to play with and against each other. The difference is that the paying players will be able to get to that point sooner. For many F2P games, there is often a difference in how someone plays and approaches these games at the late game compared to the other phases. When everyone is on the same page in terms of content, it is no longer about a battle between who has more than the other but figuring out who is the best player with the options available. There are two things you want to avoid when figuring out how to balance the game between the groups.

The first one is, can paying money supersede the need to play the game? If a free player must jump through hoops that paying players do not, then you are creating an imbalanced environment that clearly favors spending money. Likewise, if there is some super powerful item that completely breaks the difficulty of the game, but only paying players can ever get to it, then that's another problem.

The second detail is about the time that is needed in place of spending money. The point about progression in live service and F2P design is making sure that the player always feels like they're close to something new: a new power, a new unit, new game systems, etc. If the time spent to acquire something is so far off the price, free players will feel like there is too little gain for that level of commitment (fig 6.10). An example of this was in the game *For Honor* developed by Ubisoft and released in 2017. All the cosmetics and additional characters could be bought with real money, or eventually purchased with the game's free currency. However, people who examined the economy system and ran the numbers concluded that someone would have to play the game for at least two and a half years nonstop to get everything that someone could just spend money to acquire in its first year. This led to Ubisoft getting a lot of negative press and having to change the system to be fairer to free players.

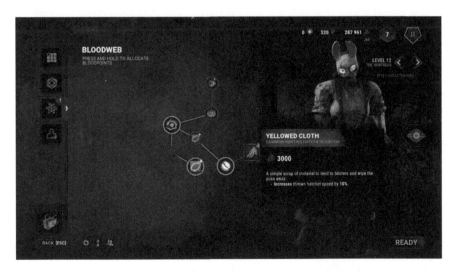

Figure 6.10

It can be very tricky to examine how progression works in a live service game and whether it is fair to nonpayers. With *Dead by Daylight* unlocking new perks and items for characters can only be done through the in-game currency (the red one at the top), but unlocking characters requires another currency that is given less, or just spending money to acquire them.

As I talked about at the start of this chapter, for a F2P/mobile game to survive it must bring in money, but how you get that money will impact the consumer base. There will always be whales who will buy everything day one, no questions asked; however, building your game to only cater to them is both highly unethical and will ruin any chance of a fanbase developing. Consumers are fine with other people spending more money to get more advantages, but if those advantages lock out others who do not, or can't, spend more money, they will grow frustrated with the experience and stop playing. I will be discussing these two points at length in Section 9.3 and talking about ethical game design.

One other point that many mobile developers have realized with the third generation of mobile, they will often be generous to free players to give them a chance at playing their game. If your game proves to be too restrictive and unfair without spending money, there is always another game out there for consumers to try.

7

The Second Generation
of Free-to-Play/Mobile

7.1 Of Brands and Battles

As with the first generation, it is hard to put an exact date on when the second generation arrived. After the success of the games that populated the first generation, traditional gamers stopped looking at mobile games, and the market was flooded with casual games. You may have noticed back in Chapter 5 that there were no already established **IPs** mentioned that managed to succeed at the same level as the big names during that generation. The reasons were that most of the major companies were still eyeing mobile games as an experiment, and the games that did come out from other franchises were often of low quality. As the industry saw the successes of the first generation, a shift began among the major studios and copyright holders to try and get into this new market.

The second generation of mobile/F2P is defined by several points. First, major studios throwing their weight, and their IPs, around to mobile game companies looking for a competitive edge (fig 7.1). Studios know that building games around famous franchises and IPs can be a moneymaker to attract those fans to try a new game out. This is the exact strategy that the MMOG market used during the 2000s that I talked about at the start of this book.

DOI: 10.1201/9781003265115-7

Figure 7.1

The second generation became dominated by IP-licensed games, all using their branding to attract fans, no matter what the property was. Even South Park had a PvP game with *South Park: Phone Destroyer*.

The second point, and one that would prove very lucrative, is the implementation of PvP-based multiplayer. Instead of having to continue to design story-based or solo content, competitive multiplayer in its many forms provides an almost unlimited amount of content when done right. In the next section, I will talk more about what PvP brings to the design.

And for the third point, the second generation's goal was to start trying to win back traditional console and PC gamers who wanted a deeper experience. The complexity of both the monetization and the gameplay would be far greater compared to the first generation. This focus would also become a driving point for the third generation, as developers were realizing the limitations of the casual market that I talked about in Section 5.3. Instead of trying to directly compete with the successes of the first generation, we would begin to see new game designs that would become integrated with the live service and F2P model.

In Section 5.3, I spoke about how casual gamers typically stick to the first game that interests them, and in response meant that the actual mobile market was far smaller for everyone else. With the second generation, designers were trying to not only win back gamers but explore different designs that weren't already being monopolized by the first generation. The games that are going to be mentioned in this section feature deeper systems in no small part due to their competitive designs (fig 7.2). For these titles, someone can't just spend money and automatically win, they need to learn how to play the game first. With that said, these games are still inherently designed around getting money, and there are limits to how far someone can get on a 100% free account.

Game Design Deep Dive

Figure 7.2

Using IPs as the base for mobile games brought with it all the various characters that could be translated into the game. Party-based RPGs became the popular genre, thanks to the hero collecting factor, and having players take their favorite teams and fight against each other. *Star Wars: Galaxy of Heroes* is just one of the many games that followed this template.

In the early 2010s, MMOGs based on major properties were still being released, but using newer F2P design as a guide. *Star Trek Online* developed by Cryptic Studios and released in 2010 combined exploring the universe with ships out of the property with ground-based combat with your command team. As of this time, the game is still active with monetization based on buying new cosmetics and ships out of the later "Star Trek" properties. The game originally was subscription-based but was turned to F2P in 2012.

In 2011, *DC Universe Online* developed by Dimensional Ink Games as the DC-based MMOG on the market. Interestingly, the game has gone through multiple revisions of its design and monetization systems over the past decade. It originally launched with a required subscription service and the guarantee that the developers could put out enough content monthly to justify it. Unfortunately, they were not able to keep that up and the game became F2P in 2011, putting severe restrictions in terms of resource storage for free players. Besides buying quality-of-life options and cosmetics, the game released purchasable "episodes" that have their own unique storylines and new powers to use. Today, episodes are released for free, but the game still locks content and features behind its subscription model.

Marvel, who was riding very high thanks to the success of the MCU (Marvel Cinematic Universe) and being bought by Disney, would license out characters to multiple studios that would take these famous properties in very different directions. Gazillion got the licensing to make two games: *Marvel Super Hero Squad Online* released in 2011 and *Marvel Heroes* released in 2013. *Marvel Super Hero Squad Online* was aimed at children, while *Marvel Heroes* was for teens and adults. With *MSHSO*, players could collect Marvel characters made in the same style as the hit show. The game's monetization was selling players on the subscription service which would allow them to use exclusive characters and earn premium currency easier. To get premium currency, players had to spin a roulette wheel and land on spaces that paid out with gold, and they could only get more spaces if they subscribed (fig 7.3).

Marvel Heroes was designed as a MMOG; the key selling point was the vast number of Marvel characters players could choose from. Each character came with unique abilities based on their comic book designs, with monetization based on new costumes and buying new characters. The game went through multiple revisions and would release new characters based off Marvel's movie lineup. The game became a cult hit, but as governments began to take a closer look at games aimed at children, Disney decided to cut ties with Gazillion and the licensing deal ended in 2017 with Gazillion closing shortly thereafter.

When it comes to the mobile side, Marvel has many different takes available. In 2013, *Marvel Puzzle Quest* by Demiurge Studios came out for both mobile and other platforms. Combining Match-3 design with collecting different Marvel characters, the game is still going strong at the time of writing this book. The gameplay provided depth via each character having different ways of manipulating the board and the player's task was figuring out the best three-person teams to use.

Figure 7.3

Part of the importance of this book is detailing monetization practices that were targeted at kids, and *Marvel Super Hero Squad Online* was one of many games that used gambling industry tactics with its monetization.

Monetization is based on both quality-of-life features and buying more resources to be used in the game. One of the more criticized practices was having a very small inventory for the character roster. If the player did not delete one of their characters or buy more space within the allotted time, the game would remove their reward.

The year 2014 saw the release of *Marvel Contest of Champions* by Kabam. One of the first mobile fighting games, the focus is on 1 vs. 1 fights between Marvel heroes and villains. Players collected new characters via the loot box system, with the goal being to build a team to conquer the hardest challenges and get the most rewards. The mobile fighting and action genres are marketed toward advanced players due to the reflex and hand-eye coordination needed to play them. Every aspect of the game has some element toward monetization, with monthly subscriptions, buying resources to make things easier or power up characters, and, of course, buying the resource needed to open loot boxes that come in different levels of power. What's unique about *Contest of Champions* that hasn't really been replicated to the same extent is tying monetization to the progression. As the player completes the story chapters in the game, not only do more chapters unlock but they also get access to more daily free rewards and the ability to open and access higher-tier loot boxes. You cannot just spend money to see everything – you must work your way through the story to access those rewards.

The fighting itself was streamlined compared to other platforms: the player could tap or hold the screen to do different attacks. Landing hits would build up a meter that could unleash up to three levels of special moves. The depth came with the numerous passive abilities and game changing behaviors that were on the more complicated characters. There are many more Marvel games based on other designs, but *Contest of Champions* is the most popular and is still one of the most played to this day.

Not to be outdone, there have been several DC-related mobile games that offer similar designs to their Marvel counterparts. However, none of them have managed to dominate the market or outpace the Marvel games.

Japan, along with other eastern countries, is another major area for mobile games. The mobile market is huge in Japan, with reports saying that it earned 1.53 trillion yen or 13.9 billion dollars in 2020.[1] Over the 2010s, there have been many mobile games first released in Chinese and Japanese markets before being translated and released globally. I already mentioned *Puzzle and Dragons* in Section 5.1. The most popular mobile game in China is *Honor of Kings*, released in 2015 by TiMi Studio Group. The gameplay is like *League of Legends* as a MOBA but has not been released for Western audiences yet. Despite that, the game has earned over 10 billion dollars in its lifetime.[2]

Just like in the United States, popular franchises in Japan have been given the mobile game treatment over the 2010s. Anime and manga like *Fist of the North Star, Naruto, One Piece, My Hero Academia, Seven Deadly Sins* and many more have mobile game adaptations (fig 7.4). For these games, they typically feature a story straight out of the anime/manga but will let people play with characters not tied to the story.

Figure 7.4

While there are plenty of mobile games still locked to the eastern markets, the ones that have become popular in the West have received global versions like *Dragon Ball Legends*.

One of the most recognizable properties is *Dragon Ball*, which saw renewed interest following the *Dragon Ball Super* relaunch in 2015. There are many mobile games released, but there are only two available to US audiences at this time. *Dragon Ball Z Dokken Battle* was released in 2015 by Akatsuki and plays more like a puzzle game featuring the different characters in the *Dragon Ball* universe. *Dragon Ball Legends* was released in 2018 by Bandai Namco and is a fighting game where players collect different characters and form teams to fight through missions and other players. Unlike other games, it does feature synchronous multiplayer that I will discuss more in the next section.

While the most popular and profitable mobile games were live service, there were still exceptions of single-player games that became celebrated on mobile. I already mentioned several, including *Angry Birds* in Section 5.1. Games like *The Room* (developed by Fireproof Games in 2012) and *Monument Valley* (developed by Ustwo Games in 2014) did well. Puzzle games, thanks to their pick-up-and-play nature, are also popular on mobile. They are also one of the few cases where a mobile game succeeded despite having a price tag and not being F2P. However, because this book is focusing on live service games and design, I won't be going into detail about them here.

7.2 Pushing PvP Play

The second generation of mobile brought with it a new way of enticing people to play with a focus on player vs. player, or PvP, design. Playing against other players was a part of browser games and the first generation, but with the second generation there was a larger focus on tying more elements to that design. Games would typically introduce the PvP component in the middle or daily loop phase that I discussed in Section 5.5, but it will not show its full importance until the player reaches the late game.

There are two kinds of multiplayer systems – asynchronous and synchronous – that determine the complexity of the modes. For most mobile games, they use asynchronous, which means that players would not directly compete at the same time. Often, this mode worked with one player who is active fighting against another player's team controlled by the game itself. Winning will give the player points that the game ranks the top players by their points (fig 7.5). The problem with asynchronous multiplayer from a balancing standpoint is that a game-controlled team will not be able to fight as effectively as one controlled by a player. In response, developers will often favor defenders by having a time limit, and if the defending team can run out the clock, they automatically win. This also means players don't have control over who attacks them and can lead to the top players simply being the ones who can reach the top first and put up the best defending team to stop all other players. Popular examples of genres that make use of asynchronous are abstraction-heavy games like RPGs, city builders, and strategy games.

Synchronous multiplayer means that both players are directly competing at the same time, which is the standard for most multiplayer games released on

Figure 7.5

Every game that has PvP gameplay will do what it can to get people to do it, even if they have no interest in it. The most popular way is to provide resources for the top players. For those with a competitive streak, they may just play for the bragging rights to be #1 in the server. *Cookie Run: Kingdom* is no exception to this, despite the casual gameplay.

consoles and PCs. In this case, multiplayer is just the same as if both players were in the same room together, and is considered the standard way of competing in reflex-based games. Creating a synchronous multiplayer is more complicated on the infrastructure and development side of the game. As the designer, you're going to need to set up how the architecture of your multiplayer is going to work, servers for players to connect to, and a lot more that is beyond the scope of this book.

One challenge with synchronous multiplayer that is important to discuss is that it requires a healthy consumer base of players active for it to work. If someone can't find people to play against, they will not be able to use the mode. With asynchronous multiplayer, some games will put in AI-controlled opponents, otherwise known as "bots," to play against if there are no other players available. For games where PvP is required to progress, this can set up a wall for new players and essentially kill the game for anyone who is trying to play it for the first time. A concept that some games use is to focus their PvP modes at specific times of the day; this guarantees that there will be a point during the day when people are actively looking for PvP matches. Be mindful of the times set up as not having enough time slots, or have them at awkward times, may prevent people from being able to use the mode.

For games that are entirely PvP-focused, they won't have issues in terms of finding someone to play; however, if you aren't able to keep a healthy consumer base, you can end up with a lopsided community where it is difficult for new players to join, and everyone is playing the late game content and there is no one in between. In Section 11.1, I'll talk more about what this means and how it has doomed many multiplayer live service games.

Incentivizing PvP is important if you plan on using it as your late game content. There needs to be enough hooks to keep people engaged. The first way is providing the player with currency rewards. Many mobile and live service games will grant a mix of free and premium currency for players who achieve high ranks. For mobile, this is often where players who rush out ahead and stay on top can consistently earn enough premium currency that they won't need to spend money. For mobile specifically, the game may have a PvP-only currency that is used for specific rewards as a way of attracting players.

For games that feature a guild system, they will often tie PvP in with guild vs. guild competitions. Guilds will fight one another with members going head-to-head and the guild itself earning points for each victory. This is often paired with yet another exclusive currency with the top guilds earning bragging rights and a lot of resources.

Depending on the design, some titles will have their PvP set up as either a short-term or long-term season (fig 7.6). I will talk more about season-based play in Section 10.4, but for PvP games, this has been a way of providing both short- and long-term rewards. Each season, every player's ranking is reset (some games will preserve the ranking to a point based on the player's progress). For every rank the player goes up, they will earn a reward usually in the form of premium

Figure 7.6

Season play is all about how high someone can reach by the end and is often tied to ranked matches. With *Hearthstone*, players who reach a high enough rank in a season will start higher compared to lower ranked players to try to keep the matchmaking fair.

currency. At the end of the season, the higher the ranking someone gets, the more rewards they earn for closing out that season. Depending on the game, the top players may get something special like a unique cosmetic or bragging rights in the game. For Esports titles, the top players, or teams, each season may earn an invitation to regional or global tournaments.

It's important to understand player psychology when it comes to competitive modes in games – whether they are PvP-centric or as an additional mode. Competition has been proven to be an effective motivator for some to keep them invested. Therefore, PvP content has become one of the best ways to design long-term gameplay around, because for as long you have a player base, there will be content in the form of fighting each other. However, if someone is not motivated by competition, or the investment is too high for them, they aren't going to be interested in playing. This also means that if your daily loop consists of nothing but PvP content, you are going to be attracting consumers who want that and repelling those that don't.

Another point is that PvP will also bring a new issue when it comes to balancing your game. Players are exceptionally good at figuring out the best ways to play a game, and they will be more than happy to let everyone know about those strategies. In any live service game, there must always be work in terms of the **metagame**, or the best and popular strategies being used. If the meta does not change, the game will devolve into people doing the most popular strategy, and those doing the counter to that strategy, and that will be the only two ways of

Figure 7.7

When the metagame becomes fixed for a game, it can ruin any competitive aspect of it. With *Gwent*, in the first version of it, weather-based strategies were so good that it dominated the meta. No matter what the developers did, they couldn't balance it, and eventually the entire system along with the rest of *Gwent* was completely redesigned.

playing (fig 7.7). Therefore, live service games are always adding new content and changing elements around to keep the player base from getting bored. There is more to discuss when it comes to overall game balance in a live service/mobile game that I will talk about in Section 11.4.

If your game is focused on competitive PvP play as the center of the experience, such as with fighting games, you're going to need to implement a matchmaking system. Matchmaking systems organize players based on their overall skill and the number of wins to create a hierarchy. As I'll discuss in Section 11.1, you don't want your casual and hardcore players to be playing against each other, especially in competitive multiplayer. The purpose of the matchmaking system is to figure out someone's overall skill at a game and place them against players who are around their same level. This is tied into the season and ranks as a way of showing someone their overall rating at a game. For more about setting up a ranking system, the ELO rating system has become the basis for a lot of competitive games.

Player vs. player content is one of several routes that you can go in terms of long-term content, but it isn't the only one, and its usefulness will be based on the design and structure of your game.

7.3 Defining Gameplay Systems

With the second generation of mobile games, the different game systems and modes that would be featured in mobile/F2P became standardized. For this section, I'm not going to be discussing monetization systems, as that was covered in Chapter 6. This section is also focused on the popular modes seen, as there are games out there with original modes or takes on these designs exclusively for their game systems.

Just like with monetization systems, you are free to design game modes however you see fit, and a major point about the third generation that is discussed in Chapter 10 is all about standing out with different gameplay. The purpose of having different modes is to give players a variety of ways of playing, which each mode can then be extended with more content as time goes on. Another reason why developers like these modes is that each one can reward the player differently and allows them to further delineate progression (fig 7.8).

Often, the different modes of a F2P/mobile game stem from whatever your core gameplay loop is. This is where being creative can help – by coming up with different variations of how someone can play your game from the CGL, you may create something new and interesting to draw people to your game. Obviously, every game has it's "main mode"; this is the one that should be played daily and is what the progression of your game is centered on. Stages are grouped into chapters with the difficulty progressively getting harder throughout the game. To add more challenge and reward, many games will have "boss stages" that can reward more resources if someone can beat it. You don't want to make these challenges too high and spike the difficulty, as that is an example of unethical design that

Figure 7.8

Creating multiple modes of play on one hand allow players to focus their attention, but it can also set up periods of time where what the player wants to do is not accessible when they want to play it. In *Arknights*, these daily challenges are the main way of improving the skills of different classes. Other mobile games give you access to all the modes daily but limit their usage each day.

I'll return to in Chapter 9. As discussed, the reason why many games like RPG systems in their F2P/mobile games is that it allows them to indefinitely expand their content with stronger enemies and rewards. For titles built on story content, you'll still need to create and write the story of the game.

Playing the main mode should reward the player with resources that they'll need for continuing, but other modes will often focus their rewards on a specific progression system. If your game is about collecting equipment or gear to put on characters, there could be a mode that only rewards gear. These modes can be further expanded by having harder variants unlocked as the player levels up, rewarding more resources or rarer ones.

There are several popular systems that have been adopted by a variety of games. The first is the "tower" challenge and provides an endless number of resources for players who want it. The difficulty of the challenges goes up with each new floor and will have a harder encounter every five to ten floors. Players will need to upgrade their characters if they want to have any chance of completing the higher floors, and games will often list the players who have made the further progress.

"Puzzle" mode is something seen in games built on turn-based gameplay. The puzzle is a fixed layout, and the player is given specific characters or resources to try and figure out the best way of winning using the game's mechanics. This mode can also act as a supplement to the tutorial and show off advanced strategies using different characters. Unlike the tower, because these test specific tactics and ways of playing, there is often a fixed number of these.

A feature that has grown popular in the past few years has been a kind of "roguelike" mode. Like the roguelikes I covered in *Game Design Deep Dive: Roguelikes*, the player must battle through different waves of enemies, but the twist is that they can choose between different upgrades that affect their characters for the run. The further they get, the more resources they'll earn, and this mode will usually reset every day or every other.

For hero collector-styled games, while not having gameplay tied to it, a "dollhouse" or "display case" mode for your characters is another popular side system (fig 7.9). Many games will use chibi versions of their characters that are more animated and expressive to move around in these areas. Players can often buy furniture and decorations to personalize this space. Some games may allow you to do tasks, power up characters, and earn rewards based on doing things here. Of the different modes, this one should require the least amount of time on the player's part after it's all set up. From a social standpoint, games that have this feature will allow players to "visit" another player's setup and see what everyone else is doing.

Having a mode for multiple players to team up against a common enemy is another popular one. Due to how easy it is to send friend requests, and the rewards you get from these modes, many people will add friends just for the mode and never communicate with them.

To encourage daily play, many F2P/mobile games will have modes available on specific days. One thing to consider is the amount of time someone needs to spend daily on your game. If you make things too involved – requiring an hour

Figure 7.9

Depending on the game, they may attach important features or functionality to their display mode. In *Figure Fantasy*, this is how players can auto level their collection to whatever their five highest characters are at. In *Arknights*, their base mode also functions as the means to get additional resources and craft items to be used.

or more a day to keep up – it may cause people who can't commit that amount of time to quit.

For PvP focused games, their main gameplay mode will be centered on playing against other people. There will usually be a "ranked" and "unranked" mode for play. Ranked matches are factored into the matchmaking and the player's own rating at the game. Unranked play lets someone play the game without worrying about it affecting their rating, and often has fewer conditions or rules for how a match can be played.

Unlike monetization systems, where you don't want to be adding new ones to your game, adding new gameplay systems can help keep your fanbase interested in playing. The as-for-mentioned roguelike mode further up wasn't in mobile games in the early 2010s, but with the popularity of the genre growing, it has been retrofitted into a lot of new and existing mobile/F2P games. If your game is focusing on a core gameplay loop that hasn't been done before in the F2P space, don't be afraid to do something differently from other developers. When handled right, adding in new game modes can be just as big of a marketing event for your game as adding in a new popular character.

7.4 Crafting the Long-Term Experience

One of the important growths into the second generation of live service and mobile games has been a greater focus on late game design and longtail development. Eventually, someone is going to see everything that's in your game, and as I talked about earlier in this book, the goal of live service is to create an experience that people will want to keep playing regularly for the entire life of a game.

As the developer of a live service game, you need to be constantly thinking about how the game is going to keep growing over its life. In this chapter, I talked about how PvP is popular to keep people playing and competing. But even the most popular PvP games need more content added. The two "easiest" options are new maps to play on and new characters to use. Those two elements can change how someone plays a game and provides far more value than story-driven content. Each new character added will completely change the balance of your game (fig 7.10). The same effect can also be seen in deck builders or CCGs when new booster packs and cards are added.

Story-driven content is for games with PvE elements, and the complexity and difficulty of making them depends on the game. In *Payday 2*, the developer's main form of content was designing new missions to test players on, with these maps being replayable based on different difficulties or unique challenges associated to them. Mobile games with story content will often have limited-time story events that someone can play for more currency, as well as extending the main story with new chapters.

Whatever content is in your game during the tutorial and daily loop phases must have late game versions of it. For PvP, the late game version is often where guild vs. guild content comes in that I talked about in the previous chapter. For

Figure 7.10

Many games will juggle the release of new content with the additions of new characters. *Princess Connect Re: Dive* keeps to a schedule in terms of adding new story chapters and focus gacha characters.

story-driven or PvE games, they have two ways of expanding: the as-for-mentioned adding of more chapters and adding in expert-level content.

Expert-level content depends on the gameplay itself, and usually has the player facing off against stat-boosted threats that aren't seen anywhere else in the game. These fights will require having the best characters, equipment, etc., with rewards in the form of unique resources or items. Many games will use this content as a way of creating a cycle of doing the content to get the rewards needed to survive the next expert content that is added.

This can also create another form of multiplayer that is commonly referred to as "raids" from the MMOG genre. A raid is when a group of players team up to take on challenges far greater than they could individually. Raid-based content can either be done in real time with everyone fighting at once or with each player fighting the threat one at a time with any damage done persisting.

Regardless of whether your content is PvP- or PvE-based, long-term content's other role besides providing more ways to play is to give players a way of testing themselves (fig 7.11). For PvP games, these players want to see who the best is; for PvE, they want to see if their strategies and progression mattered. The players who stick around to reach the late game of a title have the greatest potential to spend money if they're enjoying themselves and is often the reason why developers focus on this group when it comes to continued support. For live service and mobile games that make it to years of support, they may add in new game

Figure 7.11

Creating new challenges that match the tone and pacing of a game can be hard, as well as providing reasons for doing it. With *Payday 2*, the death wish update created a new difficulty setting that added in new enemies while tweaking the different maps. The reward for beating every map in the game at this difficulty was an exclusive mask players could wear and bragging rights.

systems or options for everyone to use as I talked about in the previous section. Regardless of if your game is PvE- or PvP-focused, you should always have one mode that best represents your core gameplay loop at the late game.

Every aspect of your design must work with each other if you want to keep people engaged with all the different kinds of content. For example, the daily loop requires both PvE and PvP play that gives the player resources that they can spend on new gear or characters; this will give them a better chance at the expert content, and those rewards can be used in the other systems. If there is a neglected system, or weak link, consumers will not want to do something that has no benefit to the rest of the game.

Some games will change their progression systems over the course of playing or introduce new ones at the late game. This is an important concept that I will talk about in Section 11.2.

Notes

1. https://www.serkantoto.com/2021/08/12/japan-mobile-gaming-market-size/
2. https://www.gamesindustry.biz/articles/2021-10-01-honor-of-kings-breaks-usd10bn-in-lifetime-revenue

8

Studying Surprise Mechanics

8.1 Defining Surprise Mechanics

A term that was coined during the 2010s was "surprise mechanics" to define games that will give the player random rewards. This was done by mobile and live service designers, but the concept itself is far older than that.

Any video game that makes use of random or procedural content generation will "surprise" the player with different situations or item drops. With the rogue-like genre that I discussed in "Game Design Deep Dive Roguelikes," because areas were procedurally generated, this meant that someone had no idea what items they were going to find. During the 1990s, with the rise of action role-playing games (**ARPGs**), developers began to use **procedural generation** when it came to creating equipment that could appear (fig 8.1).

One of the first and most famous examples would be *Diablo* by Blizzard North and released in 1996. Developers of ARPGs would create a system that generates gear based on different factors like type, rarity, damage value, and more. This "loot table" would work anytime the player does an event that would generate an item – like killing a boss or opening a treasure chest. The attraction of these systems is that the player never knows what they're going to get, and that element

DOI: 10.1201/9781003265115-8

Figure 8.1

Procedurally generating equipment has been one of the reasons for the longevity and replayability of ARPGs. In *Diablo 3*'s case, the hunt for new gear is limited by the rigid class design, which dictates the best gear to find for each class.

of surprise will motivate them to repeat the core gameplay loop to see whatever appears next. Advanced examples would randomly choose modifiers that would enhance the gear in different ways, leading to players hunting not only for better items but those that would synergize with their build.

There is a lot that goes into content generation of this kind that is beyond the scope of this book. For the act of "surprising" the player, there are several traits that the best systems have used. The actual condition for getting drops must be known to the player, with the most common one being to kill enemies. If the player has no idea what the condition is, they're not going to feel the same motivation to keep playing. There are often guaranteed ways of getting an amazing drop used as a reward for completing something hard like a boss fight. When it comes to procedural generation, games will often have multiple loot tables based on the player's level to raise the chance that they will find better gear as the progression goes on.

It wasn't until the 2010s, with the rise of live service and mobile games, that developers began to use this concept in their monetization. There is a difference between surprise mechanics in mobile and live service games and the usage in other titles. Surprise mechanics are often tied to a system that is not directly related to the actual gameplay, such as loot boxes and gacha, which will be discussed in this chapter (fig 8.2). With the ARPG genre, the player knows that if they do X, that there will be a possible reward associated to it. In live service games, the actual surprise mechanic only happens when they spend real money or premium currency akin to a slot machine.

Figure 8.2

When developers talk about "surprise mechanics" in games today, the system is designed to reward players not directly through play but by spending money or in-game resources to possibly get something good. In *Overwatch*, the loot boxes are just cosmetic rewards that are unlocked by spending money or when the player's account levels up.

Live service games that make use of these systems will often have a fixed pool of content that is randomly chosen, with the best stuff having a smaller chance of showing up. For games that procedurally generate options, the content will be different based on what happens during the generation. What that means is that there is far more variety with what can appear when the player has no idea vs. knowing what the rarest drop is from a loot box and not getting it.

The difference between procedurally generating content and just having a random drop is that the former is about creating something at the time of the reward, while the latter is simply deciding from an already established list of potential drops. Regardless, these systems have been proven to be very effective regardless of their application.

In Section 6.4, I discussed the popular monetization options, and surprise mechanics have been paired with them to produce very attractive, and arguably, very addictive purchases. Live service designers will routinely add in new content to these systems to prevent the possibility of anyone acquiring 100% of all the goods.

If you want to know more about procedural generation, be sure to read *Procedural Generation in Game Design* by Tanya Short, and for more about roguelike design *Game Design Deep Dive: Roguelikes*.

With that said, it's time to talk about loot boxes and how this term has become one of the most hated by traditional gamers.

8.2 Loot Box

Looking at almost any live service game released in the 2010s, and even before that, there have been loot boxes as a monetization element. The idea behind a loot box is that the consumer is given a basic idea of what could be in it beforehand, they spend money to open it, and then the box reveals its prize (fig 8.3). Looking at the similarities of casino and gambling to these systems, the loot box is one of the biggest examples and the most related to the act of a slot machine. The hook of a loot box is that someone could spend very little and get something of tremendous value, much in the same way that casinos try to convince you that a jackpot is only a pull away.

The truth is that loot boxes are programmed around fixed rates, with laws established that developers must list the actual drop rates in games. Due to each country having different laws and governmental bodies regarding gambling, these changes were adopted at different times. The drop rates used by developers vary, but it is not surprising to see drop rates sometimes less than a percent for the best drops.

Being generous with the term, the original version of loot boxes could be considered booster packs in **TCGs**. Unlike loot boxes, booster packs guarantee amounts of different rarities of cards, whereas loot boxes don't have that adherence. For video game usage, early examples of loot boxes being sold would be in sports games like *FIFA 2009*, released in 2010 by Electronic Arts. Players could build their own team from famous players of popular teams by buying

Figure 8.3

Loot boxes will often give the player a variety of items while guaranteeing something of a specific rarity. For the highest rewards, like these cards in *NBA 2K21*, the chance of getting them is very low and will require a lot of openings to get them.

card packs. This practice would become adopted by different games based off real sports. When *Team Fortress 2* introduced the in-game store in 2010 that I talked about in Section 2.2, it also introduced loot boxes.

There is psychology that goes into the design of loot boxes: from the actual art design to the animations that are played based on the rarity of the items found. Later examples would inform other players when someone got one of the better drops, to convince them to try and open one. For games designed around loot boxes, a common tactic used to keep people buying them even if they're getting repeated items is with the system known as "milling." When someone gets an item that they already have, it gets automatically converted or "milled" into a specific resource (fig 8.4). This resource, when the player has enough, can directly purchase high-quality items in the game. The catch is that the cost is very high and can often require hundreds of loot box openings just to afford one highest rarity item.

Due to the often-accurate comparisons to slot machines, there have been many studies done on the addictive quality of loot boxes and whether they would be considered gambling. While developers, especially those in the mobile space, have fought against these comparisons, there have been continued studies that have linked loot boxes to gambling behaviors.[1] In 2020, there were talks regarding a "loot box law" in the United States to regulate their usage and sales in video games, but the COVID-19 pandemic caused that to be pushed back. I will be

Figure 8.4

The function of milling is supposedly to give value to duplicate or useless pulls from a loot box or gacha, but they remain a system that incentivizes mass spending so that someone can then get something they want. With the importance and functionality of cards in a game like *Gwent*, just getting one new card could mean the difference in building a winning deck. (Footage shown is from an older version of the game.)

discussing the ethics of their use in Chapter 9, but at the time of writing this book, there has not been any updates on this in the United States.

8.3 Gacha Design

While loot boxes could be traced to western developers, there is a far more potent example of this philosophy out of Japan with gacha systems. Gacha, short for gachapon, are capsule vending machines popularized in Japan. Unlike capsule machines in the United States, it's common for gachapons to have very rare prizes as their top reward, making them very attractive for people to spend money on. In the game industry, an early use of their system was in the online game *Maple Story*, designed by Wizet and first released in 2003. The system has been heavily adopted by many eastern mobile and F2P games as a more potent example of loot boxes (fig 8.5).

The difference between a loot box and a gacha system comes down to their implementation. A loot box is designed around having a set number of possible drops, with the rarest having a very low chance of dropping. The consumer is conditioned to keep opening loot boxes until they have everything of value out of it. Gacha systems are typically focused on a single drop, or "banner reward," and have a chance of dropping any character or reward in most cases. The reason why people will spend money, or "pull" on a banner, is that the featured reward has a higher-than-normal chance of being given, sometimes 50% or higher. Remember that higher chance occurs only if the consumer is going to be getting a reward of

Figure 8.5

Gacha banners are created to specifically promote certain characters and are intended to be cycled out in favor of new banners. *Arknights'* banners always feature a mix of their two highest rarities of five- and six-star units.

that rarity from the pull. Many games will have "limited" banners, meaning that the banner character is only available for this limited time and will not show up anywhere else until the banner repeats, if ever.

Unlike loot boxes, gachas have an intended end in terms of spending money. While loot boxes' rates are never altered, gacha designers will have several systems in place to try and make things a little fairer, despite having very low drop rates for their highest tier (fig 8.6). When someone is pulling on a banner, the game keeps track of how many pulls they have done, and after X amount, some games will start raising the chance of that person getting something amazing. Once they have gotten a high-quality pull, their rates will return to normal. Another popular detail is that if someone makes a certain number of pulls, sometimes 100 or more, and have not received the banner character, the game will automatically give it to them, or otherwise known as a "pity" system. I will be talking more about the rarity systems and how they are used in Section 8.5.

A rarer system that some mobile games use is purposely rewarding players who will do the maximum number of rolls. Gacha games have standardized the maximum number of rolls at one time to be ten. A few examples would be adjusting the chance of getting a higher rarity of reach ten-pull, reducing the resource cost of doing a ten-pull vs. doing individual ones, or turning the act of pulling into its own mini system of rewards. In *Dragon Ball Legends*, as someone keeps pulling on a banner, for each consecutive pull they do, they'll receive additional benefits during the summon. These can include guaranteed rarity drops,

Figure 8.6

The "fairer" gachas will have systems in place so that if someone really wants high-ranked characters or a specific character, they can get it eventually like in *Revived Witch*. However, that will still require spending a lot of resources or money to get them.

lowering the cost of the next summon, and more. The problem with these systems is that they explicitly give a benefit toward people who have the added resources and implicitly punish those who are making small pulls.

Another point, and why gachas are so popular, is that they're often tied directly to new content in the game in the form of new characters. A new character in any gacha game brings with it additional options for players to use, and unlike loot boxes, gachas are not tied to cosmetic content. Because of this, gachas pulls are priced higher than buying access to a loot box. Gacha games will typically let nonpaying players earn the currency needed for pulls to give them a chance, but for someone to try and collect every character, there is no way to do it without spending money in the game or perhaps years of playing.

Just like loot boxes, gacha systems are considered a form of gambling in many countries, and their popularity led to developers being required to list all rates and the systems behind them in each game. Whether we are examining loot boxes or gacha systems, their use when it comes to gameplay-affecting changes the progression system of a game.

8.4 Random Progression

In Section 8.1, I talked about how developers who tried to coin the phrase surprise mechanics as a positive for loot boxes and gachas were not talking about the same methodology used in other games. Games that make use of random or procedural rewards have a different progression model that I want to examine here.

In most video games, progression is tied to a very consistent progression curve. For reflex-based games, the more skilled someone gets at the game, the further they can go. For abstracted or RPG-based games, leveling up their characters, buying better gear, etc. will make them do better in the game. When progression is built around random/procedurally generated rewards, it means that the progression curve is not consistent. The attraction of games that randomly give the player rewards is that you never know when something amazing appears (fig 8.7). With that said, it also means that designers don't know the exact power at any given time in the game.

One player could get lucky and get a high rarity weapon that gives them a tremendous boost and makes the content easy. Another player may not find anything that helps them and is consistently behind and having trouble. When progression is random, it can lead to this peak and valley situation, and if someone is not able to progress because they're not getting good rewards, they're going to get frustrated and quit. This can be even more frustrating if the game is designed around a single event rewarding one very powerful item, and the player gets something that has no value to them and effectively wastes the chance.

With *Diablo 3* (developed by Blizzard Studios) released in 2012, the original loot system was so wide in terms of its item generation and distribution that many players could not easily progress. Later it was found that these systems were

Figure 8.7

Games that make use of randomized equipment drops will always have another system that is fixed in its utility and offerings so that a player is not reliant solely on luck to make progress. *Grim Dawn*, like other ARPGs, allows the player to choose what abilities they want to learn when leveling up and is separate from their gear to create a build around.

being intentionally tweaked to incentivize use of their "auction house," where people could buy and sell items for real money.

When I talk about ethical F2P design in the next chapter, a big part of it is making sure that the game is fair for all players. Many gacha and F2P games will have intentional spikes in the difficulty that will often require players to have better characters/gear or spend money on their gachas to hopefully get them. With *Diablo 3*, the player base responded so negatively toward these systems that the developers had to completely rebalance the game and remove the auction house in a later patch.

In gacha-styled games, part of the balance that developers must figure out is how necessary the best units are for succeeding in the late game (fig 8.8). Over the 2010s, developers have gotten smarter in terms of designing content, and instead of it being about getting one character, it's about building an effective team, or pool, of characters. In this regard, the game is both better and worse compared to some of the simpler designs seen in mobile. It's better because no one character will make or break someone's time, but it's worse as someone is going to need far more to compete.

There should always be set systems in place that can be used to help someone when they're not getting lucky otherwise. Being able to upgrade gear and already-obtained characters to higher levels can help someone. This is also why in the previous section that gacha designers will give out small amounts of their gacha currency, so that even if someone is not getting the very best characters, they can still build a team with what they have.

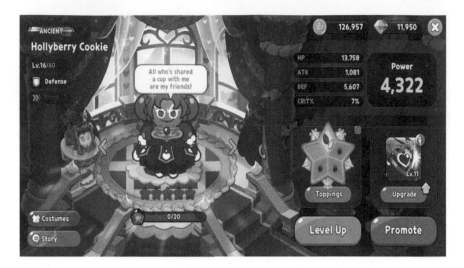

Figure 8.8

The whole point of randomized progression with gacha is to tease the chance of getting a highly valued character. To balance this, many games will make their best characters, like Hollyberry here, the hardest to get the necessary materials to ascend them, allowing weaker units to be powered up stat-wise to compensate. However, the utility that higher-rated characters bring becomes more important than just stats the further someone gets into a game.

8.5 Hero Collector Design

The culmination of loot boxes and gacha design can be seen in the style of game known as "hero collectors." A hero collector is not held to any one genre and can be applied to many different designs.

A hero collector is in a way an extension of the champion model seen in MOBAs. Basic examples will often flood their games with many different characters, while advanced ones are about more unique individuals. These games feature a standard setup by giving every character a set of basic abilities – attack, move, etc. To distinguish them from one another, they are then given special abilities or powers unique to them. Characters can belong to different classes or roles depending on the design or can simply exist as their own entity (fig 8.9).

For traditional/retail games, this is seen the most in multiplayer games. *Team Fortress 2*, which was already discussed, is a class-based design but not a hero collector. Popular examples would be games like *Rainbow Six Siege* (developed by Ubisoft Montreal and released in 2015), which continually had new characters added, and *Dead by Daylight* (developed by Behavior Interactive and released in 2016). The popularity of this design stems from providing the player with different characters that can suit specific playstyles. No player is going to enjoy every character, but if they can find at least one that suits them, they'll be able to play. This also opens monetization to adding in new characters that can give them a

Figure 8.9

Hero collector design is one of the most popular ways of designing mobile games in the current market. Every game has its own rates, kinds of characters, tier list, and, of course, price. No matter the game, from *Revived Witch* to the many others, there are people who have spent thousands of dollars in these games to get every character.

better chance when fighting other players. For these games, there is no rarity system, and monetization is often tied to either using a lot of in-game currency or buying the characters as microtransactions.

For mobile and F2P games, they are often based on popular IPs from their native country, as brand recognition is often a major selling point. For most consumers, they want to play games that let them use their favorite characters from movies or TV shows. Why play as a nameless, faceless hero, when you can control Ironman or Goku or any property with popular characters and name recognition.

In the mobile and F2P space is where the more popular monetization examples of hero collectors can be seen. In these games, every character is given a rarity rating. The rarity rating alerts the player to how desirable that character can be, and every game can have a different system. For this book, I'm going to be using the two most common designations starting with a star system. The popular number of stars is often between four and six, and can be defined as the following:

> One to two – The common or lowest-tiered characters in the game. They are often given for free to all new accounts but are quickly replaced by anything better.
>
> Three to four – The average tier that makes up the standard characters that players will get access to. Most games will give players free three- and

four-star units through play to allow them a chance at building a stable team before going after the highest tier.

- Five to six – The highest rarity units in the game. They will often have unique abilities or powers that they can only use. For gacha games, these are the characters that are used as the banner rewards. Recent examples of gacha games will give every player the chance at getting one of these characters for free when they start, but getting an entire team will take a lot of money and resources.

The other system used is a letter system that goes in this order from least to most rare: C (Common), R (Rare), SR (Super Rare), SSR (Super Super Rare), UR (Ultra Rare), and LR (Limited Rare) (fig 8.10). There can be other designations used, but it's more about the number than the names behind them. The absolute lowest that most games will go is three to have a system of okay, better, and best.

Regardless of the system used, higher rarity units will have better base stats compared to lower rarity units – inherently giving them more value and utility. There is no hard rule in terms of the number or rarity levels that should be in a game. From a balance standpoint, there should always be characters that are good enough to play with and are easy to find, and those that are far better to entice people to play and spend. One of the reasons why traditional games don't use rarity systems is for this very problem, they want every character to have value, not just anything that would be considered the highest tier.

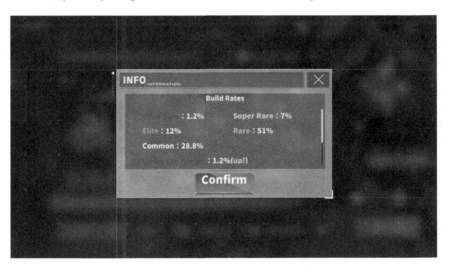

Figure 8.10

Every gacha game will have different rates for their various drops. The overall higher the rates are, the fairer a game can be, depending on the rate that people can acquire the gacha currency. *Azur Lane* has one of the higher rate chances for their best ships, and there are some games that have drop rates less than a percent.

One question that often comes up from designers is whether they should add more rarity tiers as the game goes on. This is something you want to consider carefully when it comes to the monetization and balance of your game. If a game pitches that four-star characters are the highest rarity, and then a year later five-star characters are introduced, people may see this as a cash grab. To get around this, some games may slowly introduce a new "ultimate tier" that has fewer characters in it, and new ones aren't added as frequently as other tiers. *Azur Lane* (first released in 2017 by Shanghai Manjuu and Xiamen Yongshi) originally had four banner rarity tiers of C, R, E (elite), and SR. It wasn't until 2020 that the game began to formally introduce a new tier of UR to the game. At the end of 2021, *Dragon Ball Legends* added a new "Ultra" tier to the game three years after its release, bringing the number of official tiers up to four (fig 8.11). If you are going to introduce a new tier, then you need to make that as big of an event as possible and to think carefully about how this will impact the long-term balance of your game.

To incentivize continued spending on banners, developers often introduce a progression system tied to pulling duplicates of a character. A common practice is to be able to upgrade characters using duplicate pulls of them. For every duplicate, that character becomes stronger in some way. The problem with this system is that it heavily favors people who spend money and can frequently continue to pull on banners, while free players will typically stop after they get the banner

Figure 8.11

As you design higher rarity tiers for your game, you need to come up with legitimate ways of differentiating them from the lower tiers. New powers, higher stats, new summoning animations, etc. With *Dragon Ball Legends* and their Ultra tier here, this summon also had a brand-new animation style to add to the excitement of summoning them.

character. Because of how unfriendly this system is to free players, it's important to consider how important upgraded characters in this respect are to being able to make progress and offer an alternative resource that doesn't rely on banner pulls.

One of the changes seen between earlier hero collectors and ones released today has been a focus on quality over quantity to go with the greater focus on gameplay and decision-making. Developers are not going to be releasing dozens of characters per month, as that would make it harder for new characters to stand out and for people to collect them. Most games will introduce new characters either one at a time or in a set depending on the design of the game. In-between the creation and launching of new characters, developers will often put back up preexisting banners so that players who missed out the first time can still acquire them. The general time frame for a banner is at minimum two weeks with ones for rare characters possibly lasting a month or more.

In the previous section I brought up the issue of balancing and designing a game around random progression. Hero collectors will frequently save the best abilities and powers for their highest rarity, and this can be seen in the third generation of mobile games I'll be discussing in Chapter 10. Later examples of hero collectors will place their absolute best characters behind a very long and grind-heavy set of challenges. In these examples, no one can spend money to directly get those characters, but having powered up characters through spending money will make it easier. In *Marvel Strike Force* (released in 2018 originally by Foxnext and later Scopely), the very best characters can only be unlocked through quests that require specific character types. The absolute best can be earned by completing raid-styled content that can take weeks or months to complete. *Azur Lane* has a set of missions for each one of its special ships tied to the different factions.

Many mobile games will give players who start a free character of the highest rarity to help them get started (fig 8.12). Mobile game experts will often play a game to the point of getting the free character, check to see if they're worth keeping, and if they're not, they'll delete the profile of the account and make a new one until they strike gold. As an alternative, many gacha games today will let new players make a large around of pulls on the starting banner, sometimes 20, but could be as high as 100. When the pulls are done, the player decides which one to keep, and the rest are discarded.

The more popular hero collectors on the market are always about building teams, as I mentioned in the previous section. Because they are team-focused, there is not a single character that will make you the best player in the game. Teams also provide more diversity in terms of character balance by expanding the utility options to abilities that benefit the team in some way. For games that have classes or roles, figuring out the right balance of classes on your team is part of the decision-making of playing. Games with PvP modes become a battle of whose team is built better.

From a design point of view, it is better for the long term to not rigidly define team compositions. Some games will either limit how many of each class

Figure 8.12

Starter banners like this one from *Arknights* are an okay way of giving new players a head start with their game. Having one highest rarity character is often enough at the beginning to get through most of the early content, but it won't be enough to make that account overpowered due to the focus on team composition.

someone can take or provide bonuses if someone has certain class combinations. The problem is that these elements betray the concept of team builders, letting the players create their own customized and personalized teams.

From a monetization standpoint, the problem with any hero collector-style game is coming up with a never-ending number of characters to collect. While cosmetics and personalization options are popular, it's the new characters and the utility they bring that are the best sellers in gacha games. Consumers are perceptive about what each new character offers compared to what's in the game already. As the developer, you do not want to design a character that is simply the better version of something already in the game. Likewise, a new character should not come with anything so good that every player needs that character. It always comes back to the team the player is building (fig 8.13). If I want to build a team out of fire units, and a new water unit is released, I could care less about that banner. However, if a banner comes out for a new fire unit that would complement my strategy, then that is something I would be willing to spend money and resources on to get.

The difficulty of unit creation is also why many hero collectors are built around successful and long-running franchises. Series that are ongoing provide an almost unlimited number of potential characters to add to their games. The various games built around the Marvel IP will always add new characters based on whatever TV show or movie is currently popular. Incidentally, this is often why games built around established IPs will frame their story around different

Figure 8.13

Modern hero collector games are never about one character being the absolute best, but letting players create various teams around the different styles and strategies. In *Alchemy Stars*, team composition is all about the different alignments and figuring out which one to focus on.

universes or time travel as a basic way to explain why all these characters are able to interact with each other. As a case in point, *Dragon Ball Legends* features more than 15 different versions and rarities of the title character Goku and a plot dealing with various characters and settings from the manga/anime.

One of the riskiest aspects behind balancing hero collectors, or any game with unique characters, is having to patch or update them as time goes on. Because people are spending money on characters with an intended role or benefit, it brings up the debate over changing a character for whatever reason. If a game releases and markets a character around role X, and it's so good that it begins to upset the balance of the game, removing that ability after people have spent money on it can lead to upset customers. Developers have two options: either they alter the character and offer compensation for those that bought it, or they leave it alone, which can upset the long-term balance of a game.

Hero collectors are always designed to capitalize on the phenomenon known as the "Fear of Missing Out" (**FOMO**). Consumers don't want to be told that something they want they can't have, or that they missed out on the opportunity to get something amazing. This is one of the shadier practices of gacha games and how they exploit this. Banners are always available for a limited time, and when they're gone, they may not come back for a long time (fig 8.14). Some games will transfer new characters from their banner to the general pool, while others

Figure 8.14

Exploiting the fear of missing out has been highly effective, as players not only miss out on the prestige of a character but any utility and power they might bring. When I played *Azur Lane* while writing this book, it took me about 90 tries to get the UR ship Ulrich Von Hutten.

will only let someone get that character off their specific banner. The banner is important as the chance of acquiring a specific character off banner is very low and gets even lower as new ones are introduced.

A popular tactic is to have seasonal versions of characters that are only available one time a year. This not only drives up the value of these characters but it conditions people to spend big or they will miss out. The risk of this strategy is that it can backfire if someone doesn't get what they want. When I was playing the game *Princess Connect! Re:Dive* (released globally in 2021 by Cygames), one of the best characters in the game was tied to their summer event. When I didn't get them, I felt so discouraged that I wouldn't be able to do anything for another year that I stopped playing and never looked back.

Hero collectors in their many forms work well in terms of gacha design, while providing depth and collectability for players. Remember, it's never about just having one character, but building your favorite team, or teams, of characters. These games tend to attract fans of RPG design, but there are action-based examples as well. In Section 11.3, I'll go into more detail about the balancing concerns when it comes to character design. For the games that become popular, or the developers have enough money and clout to throw around, this can lead to lucrative partnerships and collaborations that I will talk about in Section 11.4. However, despite their popularity and money-making potential, they are often the most manipulative when it comes to their monetization systems regardless of how much someone can buy. Because consumers are spending money on something that has in-game value to the gameplay, it makes these purchases more on the unethical side and provide advantages toward those with money to spend vs. those that don't.

Note

1. https://www.bbc.com/news/technology-56614281#:~:text=The%20link%20between%20gaming%20loot,and%20psychologically%20akin%20to%20gambling%22.

9

The Ethics of F2P

9.1 Anti-Consumer Practices

Welcome to the book within this book, as the topic of Ethical F2P design is one that deserves its own separate book. Throughout this entry in the Game Design Deep series, I have talked about the benefits and downsides of F2P design. These games have walked a very tight rope between simply being a game that earns a lot of money and being a gateway toward gambling and abusing their consumers (fig 9.1). Throughout the 2010s, there were many examples of exploitative F2P games by developers who either didn't know what they were doing in the space or fully well knew what they were doing and tried to fleece people out of their money.

It is no secret among people in the game industry that the companies that got big in the mobile/F2P space explicitly hired people from the gambling industry to assist with or create their monetization systems. There are plenty of mobile games that were designed around a slash and burn mentality to get as much money by exploiting people before they would shut down.

The act of designing a game to be F2P as opposed to a retail purchase means that there must be concessions made toward monetization. However, that doesn't

DOI: 10.1201/9781003265115-9

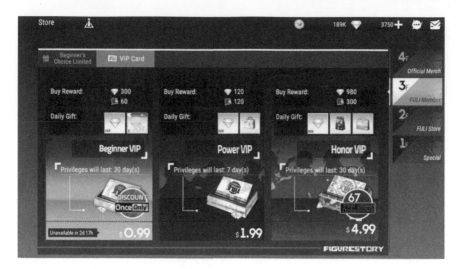

Figure 9.1

There are plenty of tactics that F2P games use that seem innocent at first but have darker motives. In *Figure Fantasy*, their beginner's VIP is a good deal at 99 cents, but if you notice, it's only available for a few days after starting an account. This tactic is not only an example of FOMO, but also gets someone to spend money in a game even before they started to really play it and start to build investment in the game itself.

excuse putting in manipulative systems designed to get people to spend money. When these monetization elements found their way into retail games, this was when the straw broke the camel's back for consumers. A game that became famous for this moment was *Star Wars Battlefront 2* (released in 2017 by Dice). In its original version, players could acquire powerful upgrades and new characters through the loot box system. However, this was not a free game, but one that cost $60 at launch and still used these systems. The backlash was huge and led to a huge negative media blitz for Dice and EA who published the game.

This led to the adoption of the term Pay 2 Win as the unofficial worse way to describe a F2P game. In Section 9.3, I'm going to discuss why this term isn't as easy to use as people think it is. Anti-consumer practices come in many different forms in F2P games. Some of the ones I've talked about already in this book include having major content only available by spending money, confusing the player with different purchases, incentivizing purchases with VIP systems, and loot boxes and gacha design in the last chapter.

There are subtler examples that can be hard to spot if you're not familiar with F2P and game design. Having intentional difficulty spikes is a common one. Games are known to have sections that are harder than others, but many mobile designers will push this too far. You can tell when a spike occurs when the content before and after the spike is nowhere near as difficult. For games with energy

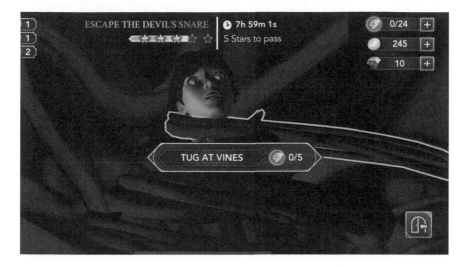

Figure 9.2

Designers have often relied on psychological manipulation, especially in games aimed at kids, to get them to spend money. In this infamous screenshot from *Harry Potter: Hogwarts Mystery*, the game is purposely set up for the player to run out of energy right when they get to this scene of a child being strangled. If they don't spend money to get an energy refill, they get to watch this child being choked by those vines.

resources, the game may be purposely set up to have the player run out at an in opportune time and try to get them to spend money to immediately keep playing (fig 9.2). An example that almost every mobile game uses is giving the player enough premium currency to make a purchase at the start to get them conditioned to the advantages of spending it and normalizing it as a part of playing.

Games built around PvP content have the potential to be the most exploitative, and why so many mobile/F2P games are structured around it. In 2017, Activision was granted a patent for a monetization-integrated matchmaking system.[1] Matchmaking systems are designed to match players with those of comparable skills and is an essential part of cultivating the different kinds of players that I'll talk about in Section 11.1. What Activision did was come up with a system that not only considers someone's skill level and play-style, but also what they purchased and how much they've spent in the game. The system can match people who haven't spent money with those who did to show the nonpaying player what they're missing. The system also tilts the experience for people who spent money so that they perceive that they got good value out of their purchase and will continue to spend more.

In other PvP games, the pressure to spend money can also come from other people playing. As I talked about in games that feature guild vs. guild content, any weak link in a guild can bring down the overall ratings and rewards the guild can earn. The very best guilds in these games will typically require players to not only commit to a certain amount of time spent per day but make sure that their characters and contributions are as high as they can be. Developers can further exploit this by designing characters that are built exclusively for PvP advantages – making them required for high-level guild play and turning those that don't have them into guild pariahs.

Most F2P games that have monetization elements don't start out with these issues upfront, but as someone moves through the different stages of mastering the game, any aspects that require money to keep up will make themselves known. To the consumer, they will most likely not notice these issues until they are far into playing a game – the daily loop or late-game phase. This is done on purpose to build that level of investment and weight with the player before throwing up pay barriers.

9.2 The Psychology of Microtransactions

When people talk about unethical or "dark-side" monetization elements, the application and psychology of microtransactions are a focus. Many F2P designers do whatever they can to push microtransactions into their game design. The entire concept behind F2P games is to not have that initial price barrier compared to retail games that can cost upward of $70 in today's market. But when you look closer at the money that can be spent in a F2P game, it is often far more than the top of a retail game.

I mentioned gacha and loot box systems in the previous chapter, and there are plenty of stories from gacha games of people spending hundreds, or even thousands of dollars, sometimes all at one time, to get something they want (fig 9.3). Defenders will often say that the higher spending occurs lifetime as opposed to at the start, but that does not excuse how these games try to condition people to spend money. In F2P games, developers will do what they can to create excitement and joy before, during, and after someone spends money. A purchase could be defined as a "special deal" or "limited time only" to capitalize on FOMO. In *Marvel Contest of Champions*, the developers will always target someone who just got a rare character with a limited time offer to spend money on resources specifically for that character class the second after they get them from a loot box.

Like slot machines before them, gacha and loot box games will have beautifully designed animations that play during the opening. Even more than that, there may be specific tells during the opening that will hint at what rarity they will earn. In *Dragon Ball Legends*, the game features multiple animations, including "fake outs," where someone will get a higher rarity than previously indicated by the animation. These animations, the buildup, etc. are all about making them appealing and to give someone a dopamine response. Dopamine is a neurotransmitter that is released when someone is doing something pleasurable. If you do something that makes you happy, of course you're going to keep doing it. For gamblers, and by extension gacha players, it's not just about getting that jackpot

Figure 9.3

Gacha games have made the most money in the mobile market in no small part due to getting people hooked on acquiring the best characters. With *Genshin Impact* and the low rate of getting a five-star pull and seeing this animation, there are whales who have gone over $1,000 on a single banner to get a character.

or amazing character, but the anticipation and build up that goes with it. While dopamine in controlled doses is good for the brain, a constant stimulation of it has been known to lead to health issues such as stress, problems sleeping, and more.

Another goal behind microtransactions is about building "investment" in the game itself. In Section 6.5 I talked about how people value time and money. Once someone has spent either a long time or a large amount of money in a game, they have now invested something into this game. It's not just something that they can uninstall or stop playing as it will feel like they have "lost" their investment (fig 9.4). A common practice is to try and keep someone interested enough in playing a game for at least two weeks, as if they're still playing by then, they're most likely going to keep playing and have that investment. Whichever value goes up first will often lead to someone doing more with the other.

To feed that addictive nature, many mobile and F2P games will have a "beginner's purchase," – something with value way beyond its price tag, but it's only available for new players and for a short period of time, like two days. It doesn't matter if it costs $5 or 99 cents, the goal is to get someone to spend money, because once they've put even a few cents into the game, just like with gambling, it becomes natural. No one ever loads up a game for the first time and immediately spends $10,000 on it; there needs to be that feeling of investment: that the person is getting something important out of playing the game. Once that hits,

Figure 9.4

The more someone spends in a game, whether it's time or money, the harder it becomes to get them to quit the game. Many games have attractive deals that are either one time or monthly to get them to spend.

spending a few dollars here and there doesn't sound like a big deal, and they'll keep doing it.

If everything in this chapter so far sounds like a huge problem for F2P and mobile games, that's because it is, and how Section 9.5 is so important to explain why.

9.3 Ethics in Game Design

When I said that this chapter could be its own book, the next two sections are the reason why. Talking about how ethics apply to game design is a topic long overdue for the industry and the consumers. People who either hate or love monetization will defend their positions to the death without understanding the bigger picture. Free-to-play design and monetization systems are not inherently "evil," and has provided long-term benefits to developers who make it work through a live service model, and consumers with games they can keep enjoying for as long as they want.

Video games by their very design are addictive, let me say that again: *Video games are addictive, and that is perfectly fine* (fig 9.5). The best video games out there are as compelling to experience as reading an entire book in one day, binge-watching an entire season of your favorite show, and so on. If something gives you happiness to do it, you are going to keep doing it. The problem is when a game is designed to demand your time, force you to play it, and keep playing beyond what you feel is acceptable. When someone becomes conditioned to keep playing no matter what, and to spend money over their limit because they feel that they

Figure 9.5

Great video games are by design going to keep someone engaged and wanting to play more. When this is coupled with a fair monetization system, it can provide a great game with years of content and support, like *Rocket League*.

need to do it, that's when designers cross a dangerous line. For a game to succeed and for a developer to stay in business, there must be profit generated. Asking a developer to release more content over years for free is too much. Developers should be making money off their games and the content they develop, but they shouldn't, and don't deserve, literally all the money that someone owns or by manipulating someone into spending.

Throughout this book I've used the term "Pay to Win, or P2W" to describe the negative aspects of F2P design. The notion of P2W is the first important part of this section, but this is not the only aspect behind ethical design I want to focus on. A game is considered P2W when there is a noticeable, and often game-affecting, difference between those who spend money vs. those who don't. Returning to Section 6.5, nonpaying, or free, players need to feel like they have a chance at succeeding. If the difference between success and failure comes down to someone spending more, that right there is an example of P2W.

The problem with consumers is that they are often quick to label any microtransaction as P2W, which muddies the discussion of ethical game design. Today's developers have learned from some of the most egregious examples of P2W design. You're never going to find a game released in the market that literally will have a price tag on the very best content, and the first one to get it will become the top player. Many games that have P2W elements in them are about using money as a shortcut where nonpaying players must jump through hoops to accomplish the same task. If it can take months to get the very same content that someone can spend money to achieve instantly, that is P2W (fig 9.6).

Figure 9.6

The more advantages spending money gives someone in a game, the more P2W a game becomes. In *Marvel Strike Force*, one of the best characters in the game can only be unlocked via very specific combinations of character types that a free player would probably not have access to at the level required when the event first showed up. This gave paying players a huge advantage that continued with their future character and team designs.

The difference between that and the gacha system is that both nonpaying and paying players must deal with the same low rates. Theoretically, a free player could get something that took another player hundreds of dollars to get. In several gacha games I played while researching, I managed to get the best characters in the game, and even one time, two on the same pull without spending one cent. However, it stands to reason that the more times someone can pull, the greater the chance of getting what they want. Likewise, once someone is in the late game content, they are going to need great characters and it is possible they won't be able to afford any more.

When a game is designed to take advantage of spending money and punishing those that don't, that is a subtler example of P2W design. Returning to *Marvel Strike Force*, the design of the game shifted after its initial release. The first iteration was about coming up with teams whose abilities would synergize or just having your favorite characters fighting together. A year after its release, the game tilted its balance toward giving teams of similar characters synergy bonuses, and even changing the dynamics of their powers if a specific character was on their team. What happened was that the high-level play was about collecting entire teams that had different roles, and you were punished in terms of difficulty and PvP for not fielding them. This went a step further when they would release teams who the most important member could only be unlocked by having characters from a previous team's release. Due to how the game gave out free resources, it was impossible to get these characters on release if you didn't spend money. For the people who did, they would have access to powerful teams for months ahead of everyone else.

Putting a metaphorical wall between what nonpaying and paying players can access is an example of unethical game design. What makes this insidious is that it removes any connection to the actual play or skill of the person involved – if someone has more money, they're going to be able to compete better than someone else. There is a difference between a paying player having more options but still losing to a skilled player who spent less and had a better strategy, and a game being designed that people who spend money automatically are going to have a better time (fig 9.7).

One of the first F2P games I played in my life was an arcade golf game called *Albatross* 18 in the United States and *Pangya* around the world (developed by Ntreev Soft and first released in 2004). Paying players could acquire golf clubs that had further ranges they could hit a ball. As a nonpaying player, even if I was the best at the systems of the game, there was no way I could compete against someone who can hit the ball in one shot the same distance that would take me two or three. Naturally, this difference would become even more restrictive the further someone gets, and the courses become longer.

When I spoke about PvP design in Section 7.2, I mentioned how games will reward the top players with exclusive bonuses and premium currency. Many F2P

Figure 9.7

The competitive fighting game community has taken a hard stance on any kind of monetization that would supersede skill. They are fine with adding in new characters, like in *Mortal Kombat 11*, but that's only because it still takes player skill and mastery of the game to win, not just spending money to get all the characters.

games are set up as a "rich getting richer" experience. People who spend a lot of money upfront can get so far ahead of other players that they won't need to spend more, thanks to getting free resources for being the top players. This leaves them in a position where the game is giving them all the currency they will need for the future, making it easy for them to stay on top.

As a quick aside, this is also where I must call into question developers who promote their F2P games as an Esport stating that "anyone can play at the competitive level" or "no one spent any money to compete." Just because someone is not spending any money now doesn't mean they didn't spend a lot at the start to get an early lead. And for the people who are truly free players, it brings up the question of how long did it take them to get the necessary content to compete compared to a paying player?

The problem with talking about ethical game design is that people get hung up on the notion of P2W and think that is the only metric, or again, all monetization is equally malicious. In the next chapter, I'm going to look at games that feature extensive in-game monetization, but still fall on the ethical side. One of the reasons for this chapter is that ethical game design is not solely about avoiding P2W elements.

A controversial monetization tactic over the last decade that I've talked about is the use of cosmetics or personalization as a monetization system. A problem with only defining a F2P game as good or bad via P2W is that it ignores the impact and potential of cosmetics as an abusive system. Developers and defenders will say that because cosmetics offer no gameplay-affecting value, it should be fine to make them only purchasable. As consumers, particularly kids, have grown up with F2P design and mobile games, cosmetics *do* impact the experience and social aspect of these games.

First, people do want to stand out and can develop a personal connection to their character or **avatar**. There is a difference between having special costumes vs. locking basic cosmetic options behind a pay wall. The other aspect is the social impact this has on kids playing with each other. Many F2P and mobile games are built to be attractive to kids, which having abusive monetization aimed at them is unethical as is. Kids have less impulse control compared to adults, and trying to get them addicted to these elements at a young age has led to much of the talks about regulating these elements in the game industry.

For these games that lock any cosmetic to paying money, it can create much of the same social stigma as a child who doesn't have the most expensive clothing or the hot new toy with their classmates (fig 9.8). There have been cases reported of kids bullying one another over someone who only has the default skins in games like *Fortnite*.[2] It is a common practice to not only lock cosmetics this way, but to also design the default skins to be purposely drab or boring compared to the paid ones to incentivize the spending.

Unless you study game design and monetization systems, it is hard to spot the warning signs when a game would fall into unethical territory. While games can present monetization elements from the start, there is often enough free currency

Figure 9.8

Personalization is a very effective form of monetization, but it has become an exploitive tactic by designers to keep people spending. Games like *Fortnite* continue to introduce new exclusive skins for limited-time content aimed at kids, and this can create pressure to get them or stand out among their peers.

and new player rewards to keep spending in check. When we begin to see these issues is when those early rewards are gone, and players are left with only what is given to them daily and the rate at which they can progress or unlock new content.

This section so far has only dealt with F2P and mobile games, but the same practices have appeared in retail games over the 2010s that I talked about in Section 9.1. Examples like *Star War Battlefront 2* or *Diablo 3* with their gameplay and progression purposely adjusted on the side of getting people to spend even more money in their games was a testbed by the designers and publishers to see how much they could get away with. Thankfully consumers did push back, and those systems were amended, but that hasn't stopped other retail games from still using loot boxes and the same elements that mobile and F2P designers have been doing. The industry has had a long-standing issue in this respect in terms of providing content that is fair to consumers while still allowing companies to stay afloat. And it is for that reason why I feel that defining what is ethical game design is an important step forward.

9.4 Defining Ethical Game Design

Creating an ethical guide for game designers to follow is a tall order. If I were to get into semantics, every game would be considered P2W because retail games have that initial price barrier. For this subject, I want to talk about what conditions should be honored by the developer for their game to be considered on the ethical side and put a term out there for people to use.

In the previous section, I mentioned that there is often a misconception surrounding F2P games as being inherently good or bad from the start, and why people use the line of F2P vs. P2W. Putting them on a spectrum, it is very rare to see a game that is either 100% F2P or 100% P2W. There are a few P2W examples that tried to experiment this way, including one where players had to literally spend money to get more bullets in a first-person shooter. For 100% F2P, these would be titles that were sponsored by governments or groups to promote or raise awareness for a specific issue and were funded to be released to the public as opposed to a product being sold.

As I said, at the end of the day designers need to get paid for the work they put into a game (fig 9.9). A F2P game that is so free that no one ever spends money while developers put more work into it is going to bankrupt a studio. This also goes for any game that is trying to transition into long-tail development like *Team Fortress 2* did following its success. In a design talk[3] from the Game Developers Conference by Valve's Joe Ludwig in 2012, he spoke about how the company had a problem with balancing the desire to make more content with the amount of money it would take. The income that was earned from someone just spending money one time (the initial purchase) was not going to be enough to finance months and years of additional content. If they were going to continue

Figure 9.9

Team Fortress 2 is one of the few examples of a game that succeeded as a F2P game while still being fair to nonpaying players. At the same time, Valve would have not supported the game at that level without income continuing to come in. As a developer, you need to weigh the work you're putting into a game vs. the amount of money you expect to get for it.

to support the game and make something to hold consumers' attention for that time, going F2P and changing their monetization was the only feasible solution.

I have a new term I would like to introduce in this book as a way of describing a game that is on the ethical side of its monetization and that is "**player-friendly design**" (PFD). In the previous section, I mentioned about the wide line between 100% F2P and 100% P2W. With PFD, this would be as far on the F2P side as a game can be while still providing continued revenue for a game. For a game to fall on the ethical side of F2P and be considered an example of PFD, it needs to address the following four points correctly.

9.4.1 Does the Player Feel Forced to Play the Game?

The first point itself is not directly tied to the act of spending money but is still considered unethical behavior that mobile/F2P games have done. When I've talked about monetization and content in these games, I've brought up the concept of giving weight to these games – that the goal is to make the game someone's regularly played game. In the first section of this chapter, I mentioned that video games are inherently addictive and that is fine when a game is good, and someone can stop when they want to.

The problem, and when this becomes unethical, is if the game directly or indirectly punishes the player for not playing. One of the most popular mechanisms to incentivize daily play is with the use of the daily loop itself (fig 9.10). When this

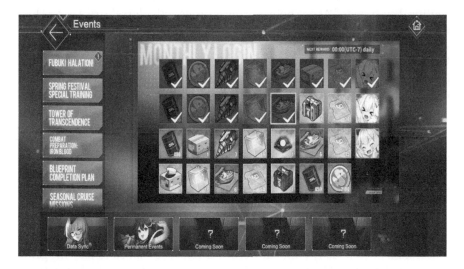

Figure 9.10

The daily login/loop in of itself can be considered an exploitative system depending on what's being given and how long it takes to achieve. With *Azur Lane,* this is the primary way to get gacha currency among other resources. However, thanks to auto-play and the tasks required, it is possible to complete every task within 10–20 minutes each day.

becomes an issue is when the daily loop becomes more and more consuming of a player's time, which often happens when they reach the late game portion of play.

Any day that the player doesn't log on is a missed day of essential resources. For free players, this may be the only way they can earn a reasonable amount of premium currency. An alternative would be to set up weekly or even monthly goals that are far easier to budget into someone's time compared to daily play. A better system that some games use is that daily goals are pooled and collected over a small window of time, usually three days. If someone wants to log in daily for their goals, they can do that, or they can play every three days, finish the goals, and then take off from the game without missing a beat. The point is that you should not be forcing someone to play that goes against their own schedule.

An indirect way of punishing is for games that push the daily play onto guild-based activities. There are plenty of hardcore guilds in mobile/F2P games. The top-ranking guilds often have strict rules in terms of how much you should be playing, what content you must do, and even how much you should spend to keep up. Any game that has guild-based content will do what it can to push players into guilds, such as having resources only available from guild content or locking out modes if they're not in one.

The social aspect of playing MMOGs has been one of the most effective ways at retaining players that I talked about earlier in this book. For mobile/F2P games today however, it has been weaponized to keep people playing. If someone isn't logging on daily to do their quests or participate in guild content, then they are "failing their friends." At one point during my time with *Marvel Strike Force* I had to not only log in daily for quests but also participate in raiding guild missions, and every other day I was supposed to set aside time for guild vs. guild content. What started at around 30–40 minutes of time to complete these tasks turned into over an hour with the guild content. It got to the point that I couldn't keep up and was kicked out of the guild even though I was still playing the game daily.

In Section 7.2 and discussing PvP games, I brought up titles that would have content available only at specific times a day. This is another example of forcing someone to play a game and alter their schedule accordingly. Not only does this fall on the punishing side, but it can also be far worse depending on time zones. When I was playing *Marvel Puzzle Quest*, their PvP tournaments would frequently end around 5 or 6 am ET, so if I wanted to reasonably compete, I had to either spend money to protect my teams or stay up that late to defend against attackers.

Returning to *Team Fortress 2*, what I liked about their item drop system was that it wasn't tied to daily play, but weekly. If someone wanted to play the game for longer than the 10 hours of possible item rewards, they could, but nothing would punish them or hurt their ability to enjoy the game if they didn't play.

Another aspect of this is the UX of a game and how easy/quickly it is to do daily loop play. Giving players the ability to quickly do daily content, or simulate their results, can cut down on the amount of time needed to spend daily on a game. While this may seem like removing the need to play the game, remember that daily content is something that is going to be done quite frequently, and can become a chore if the player is literally doing the same thing each time. In my opinion, the time to complete the daily loop of a game should ideally be around 30 minutes a day, and at most, one hour. The goal is you want the player to play the game more if they want to, but they shouldn't be forced to play the game for extended periods daily.

9.4.2 Does the Player Feel Coerced or Pressured to Spend Money?

The goal of healthy or ethical monetization is to create a game that consumers want to spend money in as opposed to the feeling that they are being forced by the design of it. In the *Team Fortress 2* presentation, Joe discussed that you cannot just use monetization systems to save a bad game – the game must be both good and with a design balanced around monetization for it to work.

Far too many designers over the 2010s have used monetization to make players feel like spending money is the only way to proceed (fig 9.11). There are multiple first-generation mobile games that tried to create arms races between the top players to keep them spending. There should not be any intentional difficulty spikes designed to punish people who don't spend money, or the game's balance being tilted to make people more likely to spend money. A common tactic of mobile developers is to purposely have difficult content just before unlocking something major to try and force that purchase. Likewise, releasing content with the explicit purpose to create an arms race scenario is also a problem.

Figure 9.11

Middle Earth: Shadow of War's original design locked the game's true ending behind a huge difficulty spike for the final chapter. If someone wanted to complete it, they would need to spend a long time grinding or feel forced to open loot boxes for better characters.

One of the worst examples of pressuring someone to spend money is giving the player something but explicitly preventing them from using it unless they spent money. In the game *Age of Empires Online* released in 2011 by Robot Entertainment, players could unlock upgrades for their troops and buildings by completing quests. However, unless the player bought the faction they were using, all the best items they would find were locked from being used. Not only that, they would also take up storage space that there was a limited number of for free players. For games with subscription bonuses, tying the use of specific content to keeping the subscription active would be another example. If the player buys or acquires something in a game, there should never be a situation where the game will forcibly take that away from them.

In the previous section I brought up how cosmetic items can impact someone's experience and be used as a form of peer pressure for kids and even adults. If the game has systems or elements designed to make someone feel bad or a lesser player for not spending money, that is another form of manipulation that is not ethical. This is also why the monetization-tilted matchmaking system that Activision patented is a big deal. If a game purposely puts players who don't spend against those who do with the intention of making them feel bad for not being able to compete, that is ethically wrong in my opinion.

As another point, the player should never be uncertain about what a purchase can give them. If a game allows someone to buy a character or a new expansion pack of cards, they should be given information as to what these options provide. This is also where games that have multiple different currencies are frowned upon for the confusion they bring. And, of course, accurate drop rates should be easily seen and shown for any loot box or gacha-styled purchase.

For a game to be considered PFD, it must avoid making someone feel like spending is the only way forward. There must be enough ways for free players to make progress, and that the free content is good enough that it will allow someone to keep playing. Someone should never feel that they lost in PvP or is stuck because they didn't spend enough money.

9.4.3 Does Spending Money Give Players Exclusive Access to Unique Content?

The balancing act that I've talked about in this chapter is that developers need to find a way to earn money through their game or they're going to go out of business. That means walking a line between having microtransactions that are worth spending money on, but not being so good that it pushes away or punishes nonpaying players. For a game to remain ethical, there should not be any system or form of content that is exclusively locked to spending real money (fig 9.12). Some mobile and F2P games will have an exclusive shop or special privileges that are only accessible with real money. I brought up the concept of VIP systems in Section 6.4, which would be an example. In *Marvel Contest of Champions*, players could subscribe monthly to access a specific store where the best items were only available to them.

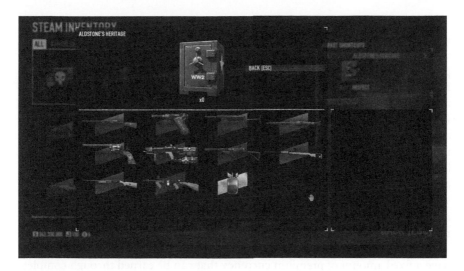

Figure 9.12

The controversy in *Payday 2* happened when the game implemented loot boxes in the form of "safes" as a form of weekly rewards like in *Team Fortress 2*. However, while *Team Fortress 2* did allow people to buy keys to access them, they were still a part of the free drop system. Before Overkill changed things, the items could only be earned by spending money.

Returning to cosmetics, this again brings up the fact that cosmetics should not be only accessible for paying players. It is okay to sell cosmetics, but there should also be some made available to free players beyond just a seasonal event deal. If there is a currency only for cosmetics, then nonpaying players should be able to earn it. There is something off when someone who is one of the best players at the game has 100 times more free currency than anyone else but literally cannot use any of that for cosmetics and is stuck with the defaults unless they pay money. Returning to the point about personalization, for any games where the player can create an avatar, there should be enough options for people who identify with masculine or feminine traits to create a character of their choosing and not lock something as foundational as body type to microtransactions.

This section is one the areas where *Team Fortress 2* excelled at compared to its peers. The item drop system that rewards players with new items on a frequent basis was the only example I could find that would give players cosmetics as well as gameplay-effecting content. And, of course, if someone really wants an item immediately, they can go to the store and buy it outright. However, there is one detail I think Valve messed up with *Team Fortress 2* – a free player would never get a key drop to open a loot box, they could only get them by spending real money. This practice has a similar psychological practice as giving the player something and threatening to take it away, except here, you're giving the player something, but telling them that they're not allowed to use it without spending money.

The experience of playing the game by spending money should not be fundamentally better compared to those who don't spend. If someone can just spend money to get perks during play, nonpaying players will not see any reason to keep playing. This was the problem with the first generation of mobile games and the MMOGs that transitioned into F2P. The experience was purposely made worse for free playing to incentivize buying things to bring it on par with other players. Returning to *Marvel Puzzle Quest,* they eventually added in the option to give accounts "PvP shields" so that the consumer didn't have to stay up late for tournaments. However, the shields had different lengths and could only be turned on by those that spent real money. Both the nonpaying and paying players should be able to access the same content, progress at the game, and eventually both groups should be on even footing with each other. A nonpaying player should never be in a position that no matter how good they are at the game or how much free currency they have, an entire system is closed off to them.

One point that defenders may try and argue about is that many games will have a fixed amount of premium currency that can be earned through completing quests and missions. The issue is that this source of currency is limited and once someone has gone through it all, they won't be earning it regularly. This is why many third-generation mobile games will have premium currency as the reward for completing daily quests, so that even free players can build up a reserve of it over time.

9.4.4 Can a Nonpaying Player Compete with Those That Pay?

This final point is one of the hardest to balance with any long-term support of a live service game. The longer a game is developed/supported affords the design team a chance to grow their own skills at content generation. For almost every live service game on the market, newer content will most likely be of a higher quality compared to the first set of content (fig 9.13). This is not an attempt at slandering any developers, it's just the nature of becoming comfortable with a design and getting more creative with it.

The problem is that as these games go on, can a new or nonpaying player still compete? This question is about two distinct areas – the quality of the content paying players get and the rate that a free player can unlock them. For any game with PvP components to it, there is always going to be that sense of competition and people looking for any advantage, no matter how minute, to give them an edge. You do not want to release something that has an exclusive advantage in one of your game systems, as that easily creates a situation where spending money makes someone better at the game. In *Marvel Strike Force*, one of the updates that came out before I quit introduced a team exclusively used for its guild vs. guild content. When this team was used in that mode, they received a huge advantage that no other team had. This meant that if you didn't have them, you were a determent to your guild. In the previous section, I mentioned how in *Marvel Strike Force* nonpaying players couldn't use new characters when they were released due to not being able to access them without spending money when they are launched.

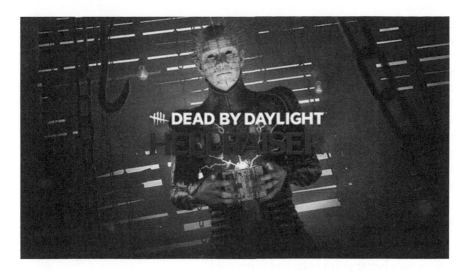

Figure 9.13

Any kind of competitive-focused live service game will always struggle with creating new content that doesn't step on the toes of previously released or free content. In *Dead by Daylight*, newer killers and collabs brought with them new abilities to stand out, and new perks that have been integrated into the meta. For new players, they're going to have trouble competing and learning the game now compared to when it was first launched.

When I talk about long-tail support in Chapter 11, I'll go into more detail about things from a balancing standpoint. For right now, new content should not be objectively better than everything else that came before it. For many deck builders and TCGs, they know that they cannot design new cards with flat out higher stats than the cards that came before, as that immediately devalues those cards and punishes players. Instead, they look at ways of introducing new elements and mechanics that keep the game growing in a new direction. Just because something is new doesn't mean its automatically better, and that very statement has often been an ordeal when trying to get feedback from players about something. A new character type or card means that the player base has zero experience using it or knowing how to deal with it.

Just raising stats higher with new content will also cause consumers to call into question whether the game can still come up with new ideas. Consumers need to always know that the developers are still working on something new and exciting. If all they're seeing is just the same content but with more stats a new price tag, they're going to lose interest. *Team Fortress 2* had a better philosophy with the side grade option, as it allowed them to tweak their characters in any number of ways, but by reducing their ability in some aspect, it meant that there was a less chance of creating something completely imbalanced with the game. Another option is to focus on team dynamics that I discussed in the previous chapter, so that balancing is built on both the individual level and what that character brings to whatever group or build it belongs to.

Some supporters of games may argue that a game is fair if you know what you're doing, or that someone who understands the systems can, in a way, "punch above their weight class" and make progress without needing the best content (fig 9.14). The problem with this attitude tends to be about two details. For people who say this, they are usually players with dozens or even hundreds of hours in the game – they know how to play the game and optimize any free resources given to them. I have watched streamers of F2P/mobile games do "F2P challenges" and see how far they can get on a free account in a limited time. One person who played *Marvel Contest of Champions* in seven days of playing made several months' worth of progress because they knew exactly what to do. Most players who play a game for free will not have that knowledge base to draw from. The other point is that there is always a limit on how far skill can go. At some point, a player regardless of their skill level is going to run into something that will require better gear/characters to proceed.

Another detail to keep in mind, if you introduce a new system or mechanic that becomes integrated into the entire game, nonpaying players must be able to access it without spending money. As a game's life span goes on, the core gameplay loop or moment-to-moment gameplay can be altered, and as a designer you do not want to put a price tag on elements in your CGL. Returning to *Payday 2*,

Figure 9.14

Arknights is a tough game to judge in terms of its fairness regarding this point. Due to the focus on planning and team compositions, five- and six-star characters do not take the place of mastery. However, the game is designed around spikes and making it harder to progress without the utility that higher-ranked characters can bring.

the game introduced a new weapon type with grenades with its third DLC. After a while and more elements added to it, the developers went back and gave everyone a standard grenade for free. For competitive games that focus on new maps to play on, given their importance to the matchmaking and competition of the game, they should never be locked behind a paywall.

For free players, new content means having to play against it with what they currently have. The longer a game is out for, the harder this becomes for new players to the point of the game almost punishing them for trying to play it today. This is where having systems in place that allow someone to be able to compete and unlock things come into play.

An example of this not working well is the game *Dead by Daylight*. Late-game play in *DBD* is about mixing perks from different characters to create customized builds for the player's character of choice. To do that, players not only have to unlock those characters but also level them to the point of unlocking that content for other characters. To purchase a character, a player must either buy the DLC or spend a special in-game currency to unlock them. Leveling up characters requires an additional currency that is only earned by playing the game. Due to how the game has been updated multiple times, it's hard to find a current and accurate statement on how long this takes, but some estimates say that it is about 35 hours per character to unlock them, and that is active hours in matches. All the while, free players will be up against those who have those unlocks and have a huge advantage against them. As a tangent, this is the reason why effective matchmaking is important in any PvP-focused design. Not every character can be purchased this way as there are some that are only available by buying the DLC or spending premium currency. And just like how character designs become more advanced, so has new perks in terms of offering more choices and value to players. With this kind of content structure, it means that every new major update furthers the divide between current players who have access to everything and the ones that don't.

Figuring out how much to price content like this is a tough question for designers. With any kind of character-driven game or buying cosmetics, once someone buys or gets access to it, that purchase is no longer an option to that consumer. However, if a game is meant to be played competitively or with a ranking/matchmaking system, if players are put into situations where they are forced to compete but can't, that creates an imbalance (fig 9.15). One solution seen from *League of Legends* is to have a weekly rotation of free characters of each role. If someone can't or won't spend money to unlock more champions, they can still play competitively and even get a chance to try out new characters. This question is dependent on the design of your game and the rollout of new content. Remember that once games reach years of being supported, the new player experience is going to be different compared to people who were there day one. There could be new systems that have been introduced, new rules and mechanics, and content that wasn't created yet. If you're noticing high player churn among new players coming in, it may be wise to change the onboarding and early game monetization

Figure 9.15

The more competitive-focused a game is, the more specific it needs to be with what it monetizes. For games with actual competitions and a Esports following, they will make it as fair as possible for players to compete on even terms. With *DOTA 2*, microtransactions only affect cosmetics and personalization, and not 1 cent can be used to affect the actual playing of the game.

and progression, as you need to have an influx of new players to create a healthy community.

If it can take months of playing to unlock content in a game compared to just spending money, that is clearly an example of a developer not valuing the player's time. If a new character or set of cosmetics are released, there should always be nonpaying players who should be able to access it given enough resources from their time playing. A newer system is the idea of a battle pass or season play that I'll be talking about in the next chapter as a way of providing all players the chance to unlock new content while still providing incentives for paying. It should always be possible for free players to be able to compete against those that pay.

When I said "to compete" in this section, it's important to clarify that. Nonpaying players don't expect to get access to everything at the same rate as paying players, but they should always be able to have a fighting chance no matter how much someone else has spent. As the designer, you need to look at what you're offering for free or purchasable with in-game currency. It's a balancing problem if the base/free content is all-around worse and not viable compared to even the cheapest paid option. The CCG genre is famous at this point for introducing new cards with their own rules and play-styles completely different compared to the base or free decks. This also has the effect of making the new player's experience worse if a player coming in has no hope of winning with what the game gives them. This can also mean changing or adding rewards for new players to give them the means of getting started on the right foot in games that are up to years of content available.

I'll be expanding on this point in Section 11.3; but from a balancing standpoint, you want every option in your game to have viability. Players shouldn't be spending money for just power, as that's P2W. Someone who knows your game inside and out should be able to win with the free options just as well as with the paying ones.

One final topic about PFD that I need to touch on for this section. From a designer and monetization point of view, you are going to need to figure out how much money you should reasonably expect from each consumer (fig 9.16). While that may sound impossible at first, once you know what your monetization system is and your core gameplay loop, you should be able to create a reasonable estimate for what people can or need to spend to enjoy the game. Earlier in this chapter I mentioned how many mobile and F2P games were set up to court whales, hoping that the 1% or less of their consumer base will fund most of the development. If you design your game with mechanisms and pricing specifically to engage with that target group above everyone else, it's going to lead to people seeing the writing on the wall and quitting. You should not be treating your monetization system and its content as an infinite well of money, but that each microtransaction having an intended limit per consumer.

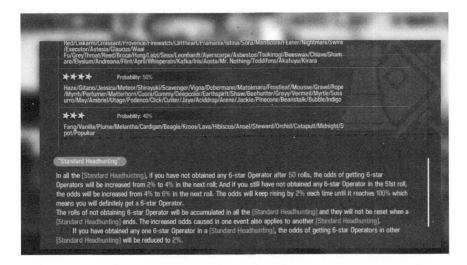

Figure 9.16

Gacha-styled games released today will have a pity system in some form or another, and while defenders will say this makes things fair, it still can require someone spending at least $100 or more in some games. With *Arknights*, it can get very expensive to get a specific character. There should be an acceptable standard for pricing when it comes to content in F2P games.

If you want your game to be considered PFD, there should not be any purchase, gameplay-affecting or cosmetic, that has no limit on spending for it. If you want to sell the player on the chance of getting something rare, there's no problem with that, but there should be a fair point where if someone is still spending to get something, the game should just give it to them, or just have a set price someone can pay to access something. That also means nothing in a PFD game that has a real money cost to get should only be accessible through a random purchase, there must always be that set price point.

9.5 Why This Matters

This chapter is one of the longest in the book and is a topic that many developers don't really think about. Everything written here could easily be ignored by many mobile/F2P designers. However, that would be a huge mistake with both the growth of the market and the overall literacy consumers and governments have about it. The number of laws and regulations around the world for mobile and F2P games in terms of how and what they can sell have changed over the 2010s. In 2012, Japan banned a form of gacha known as "complete gacha,"[4] where the only way to get the top prize was to collect a set of prizes first. China required companies to show drop rates and possible rewards for loot box and gacha systems in 2016.[5] Because each country has different laws for gambling, they would adopt similar and different laws throughout the decade. In 2020, there were plans by the US Congress to debate over a bill to regulate the design and selling of microtransactions in all video games.[6] This bill would purposely target all elements that could be conceived as aimed at minors, even if the game was marketed toward teens and up.

One of the reasons why companies have gotten away with this for so long has been the targeted focus on children. Children don't have the mental maturity to understand how the cost of something works, and parents for the longest time didn't monitor the games their children were playing (fig 9.17). Governments and gambling regulators around the world are still behind in terms of the growth and impact video games have, and why they weren't paying attention to the rise of unethical monetization practices in the game industry. And that would have most likely lasted without cause for alarm if the game industry didn't get greedy and continued to push how far they could go with adding them to video games. If gambling is considered something for adults only, it would stand to reason that games that make use of monetization systems adopted from the gambling industry should be considered adult's only due to their designs.

If the version that congress had debated did get passed and made into a law, it would have meant the literal end of the mobile and F2P market overnight. Anything that the government perceives as being targeted to minors, either directly or indirectly, would have had to be removed. This would have required developers to completely rebuild their monetization systems and the UI/UX of their titles; all the while, the game would not be making money and developers

Figure 9.17

There have been many mobile games released in the 2010s aimed specifically at children, like *Smurf's Village*, that use the same monetization practices aimed at adults that I've outlined throughout this book. And the stories of kids spending thousands of dollars without knowing it fueled the response to create legislation around mobile games and monetization.

could have been fined over noncompliance. The only thing that stopped this from being debated at the time was the arrival of COVID-19, but it is still there waiting to be picked up again.

One area where the game industry has had trouble with is when it comes to self-regulation. No one who makes games wants any governmental body to dictate what can and can't be made and sold, but the only times that the industry takes steps to rectify this is to defend itself as opposed to being proactive. There was the debate over violence in the game industry in the 1990s, which led to the creation of the **ESRB**, but that only happened when there was a threat of the government cracking down on the industry.

Over the 2010s there have been multiple stories, hearings, and studies about the impact of microtransactions and loot boxes with their addictive qualities on people. Developers and publishers alike kept pushing the boundaries of what they could get away with and continue to do so. In Chapter 11, I'm going to talk about some of the current trends that could change how monetization systems work in the future, but that's not without a warning.

If the industry doesn't come together to set legitimate standards in terms of monetization, it is risking bills like the one I mentioned being passed. While this would hurt all the bad players in the space, it does not discriminate against games that have done what they can to keep their monetization systems fair. Live service design requires monetization to continue funding and development of the game.

Without monetization, long-term support of titles with exception to a return to subscription models would not be possible. Free-to-play design, much like any system in the developer's toolbox, is not inherently good or bad, but it comes down to how it is implemented.

I have one final point to make in this chapter. Part of the purpose of writing this book is to expose these monetization practices and systems that would be considered unethical and harmful. For someone like me who studies design and understands these systems, I could make one of the most addictive, profitable, and mentally damaging examples on the market, and there are several people I know who could do the same with their knowledge. And that's the scary part, some people make games like this without understanding the greater consequences, and some because *they do* understand them.

This is not the case of doing something bad and being punished for it, the games that use these systems, but can obscure the unethical traits, have gone on to make huge profits. If these systems didn't work, publishers and developers wouldn't be rushing to add them. Games that purposely mislead or exploit people for money are the worse and negative examples of the game industry, and if the industry doesn't start condemning and moving away from them, I fear that steps will be taken by governments to shut it all down for both the good and bad parties.

Notes

1. https://patents.google.com/patent/US20160005270A1/en
2. https://www.polygon.com/2019/5/7/18534431/fortnite-rare-default-skins-bullying-harassment
3. https://www.gdcvault.com/play/1015654/Team-Fortress-2-from-the
4. https://www.gamedeveloper.com/business/why-quot-kompu-gacha-quot-was-banned
5. https://screenrant.com/lootbox-gambling-microtransactions-illegal-japan-china-belgium-netherlands/
6. congress.gov/bill/116th-congress/senate-bill/1629/text

The Third Generation of Free-to-Play/ Mobile Games

10.1 Carving Out Genres

The first generation was focused on the gold rush of casual games, the second generation was about trying to bring core gamers back with popular IPs, and the third generation is going beyond that with games designed to take over specific markets.

Over the course of the 2010s, developers have chased after different markets and game genres. By the end of the decade, the landscape for mobile and F2P design has become solidified with the games that dominated at the start still thriving, and new games trying to find their mark. For this generation, designers are giving up trying to be the next *Candy Crush Saga* or *Marvel Contest of Champions*, and instead want to establish themselves as the standard of a form of design.

While there are still plenty of licensed games being made for F2P and mobile, this generation is also made up of many original properties, with the most successful ones then becoming an IP licensed to other games. The goal is now to deliver on a gameplay loop or design and become the top dog there. The games that I'm going to mention in this chapter have very few direct competitors, and

DOI: 10.1201/9781003265115-10

that's the goal of the third generation. As an interesting point, we are seeing examples of developers taking popular genres and designs from other platforms and putting a mobile/F2P spin on it (fig 10.1). This has led to a fundamental change in monetization systems and design.

Back in Section 4.4, I posed the question as to whether any genre could be designed around live service/mobile gameplay. With the third generation, developers have experimented with more action-based designs and expanded RPG elements. There are now tactical strategy games being developed around live service, and the push for battle royale-styled games that I'll talk about in the next section. These games continue to have a core gameplay loop that is only a few minutes long but expands the content around them with more progression elements and additional modes.

From a monetization point of view, the third generation has brought with it a new focus on making the base experience of a game as good as possible and using monetization to supplement and grow that experience for people who want it. The days of releasing a mobile/F2P game with any intentional problems or pain points is over, as well as having required ads to watch. Popular monetization beyond just buying currency is now focused on premium content. This can include getting very rare characters and equipment, or cosmetics with high production value put into them. It is not uncommon in games today that have cosmetics to give them custom animations, in-game graphics, and special effects like the premium skins *League of Legends* has. Live service games today will

Figure 10.1

The third generation of mobile games has been about embracing popular genres and designs and figuring out how to create a F2P twist on it. With *Alchemy Stars*, its gameplay is like the game *Grindstone*, but with its own aesthetics, the added monetization, and live service development model.

Figure 10.2

Giving new players a free high-ranked character is a popular option to show players what the best characters can do and provide an early game boost that will peter out over time. With *Fire Emblem Heroes*, because of the importance of having different classes, one free five-star will not last long in terms of making the game easy.

frequently run special events and promotions to keep people interested and have the side effect of rewarding more resources for free players.

Even gacha games designed today have become more generous and will offer free players high-rated characters as rewards for playing to give them a chance at still being viable as they continue to play (fig 10.2). They will often let players get the choice of one highest-rarity unit of their choosing when they start up the game. As I mentioned in Section 8.5, another option is letting the player see the results of a lot of pulls, even up to 100, and then the player decides which pull they want to keep as theirs. On that note, some gacha games regularly give free players enough gacha currency to do a ten pull at least once every ten days.

It can take a long time for these games to become popularized, but when they do achieve it, they become fixtures in the market which has led to their longer-lasting appeal.

10.2 Major Mobile (and F2P) Names

It's going to be near impossible to give an accurate date for when the third generation could officially have started. Two of the games I'm going to talk about in this chapter started in the early 2010s but evolved and changed to the point where they would be considered examples of the third generation. There is also a good chance that this list will be expanded on in the future with the games released in 2021 and 2022, and with games that still don't have a global release. For consistency, I'm going to be using the global release date when ordering the games in this chapter. Of the games mentioned in this section, this is only going to be a small selection of the many mobile and live service games that have been released.

Nintendo is the company that originally popularized handheld games with their Game Boy line, and was one of the factors that kept them in the hardware business in the 2000s. The company did not look at the mobile market for the first half of the 2010s. Starting in 2016, they released and published their first mobile games with *Super Mario Run* and *Pokémon Go*, respectively. I already talked about *Pokémon Go* in Section 4.3. *Super Mario Run* combined platforming gameplay with the design of an endless runner (fig 10.3). Unlike their other

Figure 10.3

Despite Nintendo's many years of handheld and portable experience, their first game *Super Mario Run* did not do well in the market. The problem was trying to charge $10 for a mobile game in a F2P market. With their later mobile games, they did not make the same mistake.

mobile games, *Super Mario Run* was not F2P. In 2017, they would release F2P mobile versions of two of their other popular franchises with *Fire Emblem Heroes* and *Animal Crossing Pocket Camp*. Both games take the gameplay loops of their retail counterparts and introduced live service support and mobile monetization. The successes of these mobile games and other ones, along with the overall success of their portable console, the Nintendo Switch, were factors in them moving away and discontinuing the Game Boy line. The only Nintendo-published mobile game not tied to one of their existing franchises at this time was the action RPG *Dragalia Lost* in 2018, but it was announced that Nintendo is stopping content updates in July of 2022.

In the 2010s, an up-and-coming genre that was gaining popularity was "Battle Royale." Named after the movie of the same name, battle royale games take many players, typically a hundred, and drop them onto a single map with no weapons or gear. Players must scavenge for weapons and gear while the play space shrinks and the last person standing will win. Several games were released, but the first one to become a major name was *PlayerUnknown's Battlegrounds* (originally designed by Brendan Greene), or more commonly referred to as *PUBG*. When it first appeared in 2016, it was considered the height of the battle royale genre. In 2017, Epic Games released a new game called *Fortnite*, in which players teamed up to construct buildings and defenses to protect themselves from invading monsters. The game did modestly, but it would not be considered at all a commercial or critical success.

After two months of being out, the developers would release a new battle royale mode for the game. Combining the ability to construct structures with the free-for-all gameplay of the battle royale genre, it blew up in terms of popularity. The game had the best **aesthetics** for the genre on the market and the clout and resources of Epic Games to push it to the mainstream. Unlike the other Esports games at the time, *Fortnite* had a huge appeal toward kids with its cartoon-style and would go on to become a popular streaming and Esports game. *Fortnite* capitalized on many of the design trends and monetization systems that live service/mobile games would use (fig 10.4). With Epic's resources, they were putting out new content bi-weekly for a time. The game had loot boxes, an in-game store, season play and battle passes, and many collaborations. This was one of the rare times where the first game to blow up, in this case *PUBG*, did not become the standard of the genre. *Fortnite's* success created a brief battle royale gold rush of designers trying to capitalize on it in both the indie and AAA space. Besides *PUBG* that is still around, the only other major competitor at this time is *Apex Legends* (released in 2019 by Respawn Entertainment). Due to the competitive nature of battle royale games, monetization is always about buying cosmetic and nongameplay effecting content.

Returning to mobile, the latter half of the 2010s saw new games being released from eastern developers. *Azur Lane* was about combining fleets of anthropomorphized naval ships turned into anime characters to fight in an alternate WW2. Combat was about moving your ship girls around in real time to dodge incoming attacks and fighting back with your own weapons. The monetization was focused

Figure 10.4

Fortnite's fame has been instrumental to Epic's big plays in the industry. They now have their own digital store to compete with steam, and they continue to keep updating and adding new content to the game. Each season introduces brand new storylines, challenges, and cosmetics, and alters the game map. The purpose is to keep giving fans new reasons to come back and play.

on banners for new ships of the different factions and an extensive, and very risqué, selection of alternate skins and cosmetics. It is an example of a game that is very generous in terms of giving out currency for gacha pulls, but players can still buy more if they want. The real money is with the cosmetics, which outside of specific event rewards can only be bought with real money. Since its release, the game has had collaborations, an anime series, and spin off games.

One of the reasons for the growing popularity and increased depth of mobile games came with smartphones becoming more advanced (fig 10.5). There are far too many RPG-styled games on mobile released to list them all. *Epic Seven*, developed by Smilegate and released in 2018, is a party-based RPG where players collect new characters and equipment to build parties out of. The game features some of the more impressive animations and graphics on mobile, along with the depth of the party building, and has kept it as one the top games of its style.

Honkai Impact 3rd by miHoYo, released in 2018, is an action game that combines the gacha design of collecting new characters with real-time combat. Each character has different abilities they can use, which changes how someone plays and fights. It is also one of the few mobile games to be ported to other platforms, with a PC version released in 2021. Many of the design elements seen here in terms of control and style would later be adapted to their recent success *Genshin Impact*, which will be discussed further down. The market for action-based mobile games is essentially split between *Honkai* and the game *Punishing Grey*

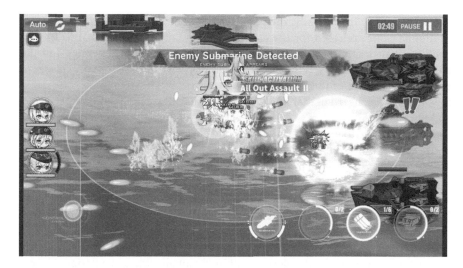

Figure 10.5

The successes of *Arknights* and *Azur Lane* (shown here) can be attributed to being unlike anything else on the mobile scene in terms of how they monetize, their events, and their core gameplay loop. At the time of writing this, there is not one game that comes close to competing with either one of them gameplay-wise.

Raven, developed by Kuro Game and released in 2021 with more games on the horizon for 2022 and beyond.

More advanced examples of strategy games were also starting to be seen on mobile. Released globally in 2020, *Arknights* by Hypergryph combines gacha-style collecting with tower defense gameplay. Players build teams of characters who are categorized by their rarity and class. The goal is to set them up in stages to stop waves of enemies from getting through. While higher rarity characters were better compared to other characters, players couldn't get by on power alone. Maps would require different party compositions and having a plan against the different enemy patterns. The skill and depth of playing combined with the gacha collection of new characters has made it very popular. Of the games I researched for this book, it is one of the stingiest when it comes to earning gacha currency, but the different characters provide more value compared to other gacha games. Since its release, it has had several collaborations, a planned anime series, and it is still going strong at the time of writing this book.

As I mentioned further up, the success of *Honkai Impact 3rd* would lead to miHiYo going big with *Genshin Impact* in 2020. In terms of scale, the game is a third-person open-world title similar in basic gameplay to *The Legend of Zelda Breath of the Wild* by Nintendo (released in 2017). Like *Honkai* before it, the different characters make up both the depth and monetization system of the game. Every character is distinguished based on their weapon preference and elemental affinity. Characters can be unlocked through the story, but the bulk are tied to its gacha system. Incidentally, the game features one of the lowest drop chances in mobile games released for the current market with its rarest characters and equipment sitting at 0.6%. Elements have different effects on enemies and the environment for puzzle solving and the open world is full of secrets and places to explore. This is one of the largest games to be released in the mobile space, and the only one I've heard of that had a simultaneous release across mobile, console, and PC.

I had a chance to play two unique mobile games while doing research for the book, with the first being *Alchemy Stars* by Tourdog Studio released in 2021. The gameplay consists of moving characters across a multicolored grid. For each space moved, characters who belong to the same element as the color will attack enemies and use special abilities. It's a similar system seen in the game *Grindstone* by Capybara Games released in 2019, but with the focus on creating teams of characters to use.

Another game was *World Flipper*, developed by Cygames and released in 2021. This is the first time that a developer combined pinball with gacha design. Players build teams of characters who take the form of the "ball" that are launched around fields to hit enemies. Each character has a super move, and progression is about leveling them up and finding equipment.

I want to clarify a point for this section. The mobile and F2P markets can change dramatically from year to year. The games mentioned in this chapter can wax and wane in terms of their popularity. Depending on when you're reading this, there could be games that are no longer popular or even shut down and not playable.

10.3 The Successes of Warframe and Path of Exile

In one of those strange coincidences for the game industry, two games that would become massive F2P successes in their own fields would be released in 2013. Starting with *Warframe*, developed by Digital Extremes. The studio spent much of the 2000s trying to make a name for themselves and create their own IP. Their first original game *Dark Sector* released in 2008 did not become a big hit. Following that and working on other projects, the studio released the first version of *Warframe*. At the time, it was rare to see a F2P game focus on PvE design as opposed to PvP.

Players controlled creatures known as Tennos, who use high-tech suits known as warframes. Gameplay is about using a variety of guns and melee weapons to fight against aliens and figure out what happened in the galaxy. Unlike other F2P or action RPGs that tended to favor slower-paced gameplay, *Warframe* became famous for its fast pace and the ability to quickly move around the map (fig 10.6). Combat was about using a combination of special powers and close- and long-ranged weapons either alone or with a group of other players.

As a live service game, it is most notable for two things: a never-ending amount of content updates, and its massive in-game store. The developers have no intention

Figure 10.6

Warframe came out at the right time to capitalize on being a noncompetitive F2P game. The game has captured the market so well and is so big content-wise that no one has tried to compete with them and is still going strong after so many years.

of finishing *Warframe*, and instead release massive expansions at least once a year. These expansions add in new story content, new equipment, and in some cases brand new systems or updating those already in the game. Since the original release, some of the new systems added included getting a war mech to use in battle, creating and customizing a new ship, open-world gameplay, and more.

The monetization system of *Warframe* is one of the most extensively seen in any F2P game. Everything in the game, gameplay affecting or not, can be purchased through the store (fig 10.7). Regarding gameplay, besides new weapons, the other factor that dictates the general play are the warframes themselves. Each warframe is like a class or champion in other games and has its own playstyle and unique abilities to go with it. You might be thinking that this sounds like a huge example of unethical and P2W design, but there is a twist here. Outside of cosmetics, players can eventually craft new weapons and warframes by exploring the different maps and gathering resources. Using their in-game 3D printer, players can create the various parts of a new warframe and eventually unlock it permanently for their account. Spending in-game currency is just the way to acquire cosmetics or speed up the unlocking process. If someone doesn't want to spend money in *Warframe*, they can still enjoy the game and make progress through all the content, and none of the expansion content is locked behind a paywall. *Warframe* continues to be a huge success and brings in millions annually and they have their own yearly fan convention known as Tennocon. As of 2021, they just released another update to the game and show no signs of stopping any time soon.

Figure 10.7

Warframe's store is an interesting case when it comes to monetization. Whether you are spending premium currency (platinum) or not, every player will make use of it for purchasing goods they need for crafting or quests. It is the largest in-game store I've seen in any F2P game, but due to the design of the game, you can in fact play through all the content for free.

Path of Exile by Grinding Gear Games had perhaps one of the best opportunities any developer had in the 2010s. A year prior to its release, Blizzard put out the much-anticipated *Diablo 3*, but a poor reception due to its balancing issues and auction house system left many fans wanting a new ARPG to play. This gave *Path of Exile* a huge marketing advantage as the "good ARPG" when it first came out (fig 10.8). The gameplay involved creating a character who was exiled to the mysterious land of Wraeclast where they must fight their way through monsters to figure out what is going on.

What separates *Path of Exile* from other ARPGs was a different focus on progression and character growth. Instead of the classes being rigidly defined in terms of their abilities and utility, every skill in the game could be used by any character, with the limitation being their stats. Each class starts on a specific area of *Path of Exile*'s massive skill tree (fig 10.9). Each node on the tree represents either a unique passive that changes the character or improves a specific characteristic. There was nothing stopping a player from building their character however they saw fit. Besides gear, skill gems could be found that were akin to the skills seen in other ARPGs. If someone wanted to give their warrior a skeleton army or the witch-heavy weapon skills, provided they had the prerequisite stats, anything was possible.

Like *Warframe*, anyone can start playing *Path of Exile* and without spending money get a complete game's worth of content to go through. This amount of content would be expanded throughout the 2010s with their own versions of season-based

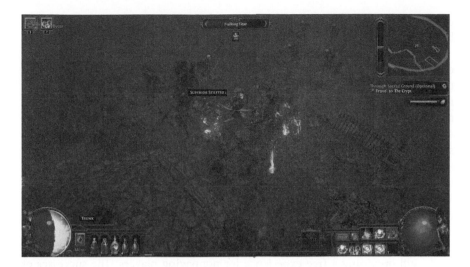

Figure 10.8

Path of Exile provided a quality ARPG experience for free and stood out in stark contrast to the issues that plagued *Diablo 3*. While it didn't have the budget of *Diablo 3*, the game has seen many updates that have kept fans playing. It is also the only F2P ARPG in the market that has done well over the 2010s.

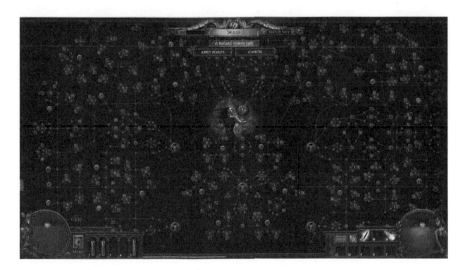

Figure 10.9

The skill tree of *Path of Exile* is something always shown to people to emphasize the depth of character progression. Like *Warframe*, *Path of Exile* is a fully featured game that can be played from beginning to end for free, and why they both stand out among the rest of the F2P market.

play, expansions adding in more content, updating the art of the game, a redesigned late-game and much more, all accessible without spending money.

Where the monetization comes in is with an extensive number of cosmetic and personalization options (fig 10.10). Players can purchase pets that can follow them, unique looks for armors, elements that change the look of the UI, content for guilds, and so on. The only gameplay-affecting purchase is being able to buy more stash tabs, but the game already gives more than what most players will need. The big money-maker in terms of cosmetics is being able to buy alternate skins for different skills. These purchases change the look of a skill, making it look and sound different, but do not change the properties or utility of it. This is to my knowledge the only game that does this specific kind of monetization. While the game does have seasonal and league content, it is completely open to nonpaying players. At this moment in time, Grinding Gear Games is working on a sequel to *Path of Exile* and in 2018 was acquired by the company Tencent.

Both *Warframe* and *Path of Exile* represent the advantages of the F2P model while still providing a free experience for nonpaying players. The successes of both have given their respective studios a major hit for years now. Neither game is designed in a way to put up a roadblock that requires money to get around. While personally I'm not a fan of locking all cosmetics to purchasable only, they are the closest to PFD compared to a lot of F2P/mobile games that came after them. There is never a point in either game where someone should feel like there

Figure 10.10

The monetization system of *Path of Exile* is a great example of coming up with interesting and different cosmetics for personalization. Many games let the player change their armor color or style but changing the aesthetics of skills and UI elements is not often seen. And even with this only being purchasable using money, the fans don't mind this, as they're getting all the gameplay for free.

is no way to progress without spending money. The fans agree on the fairness of these games, with both titles having successful fanbases who have continued to support the game with purchasing content and cosmetics.

10.4 Battle Passes/Seasonal Play

The original concept behind F2P games was to get away from the subscription-based model of the MMOGs that forced people to spend monthly for access. As F2P game design grew in popularity, a new monetization system was developed to provide the concept of a subscription with the allure of new content for players. A battle pass is tied to what is considered a "season's" worth of play and content. A season's length can vary based on the design and nature of the game – typically at minimum a month but could be longer as well. The battle pass features different tiers of content and challenges for the player to complete. These challenges range from simply winning or doing the core gameplay loop to performing specific tasks during a match. Completing challenges reward points that at different thresholds will unlock resources, a new item/cosmetic, or both. Where the subscription comes in is that players can purchase the pass which unlocks a higher quality version of it. The purchased battle pass will always have more exclusive content and premium resources and will give out more as a whole compared to if someone was to buy everything individually (fig 10.11). For the content itself,

Figure 10.11

Season and monthly passes have now become a mainstay in F2P/mobile games since the mid-2010s. With the amount of content and rewards possible to earn from a battle pass, a consumer can get incredible value out of it for the games they love to play. With *Dead by Daylight*'s battle pass, the amount of premium currency you spend to unlock it will be earned back, along with other rewards, for players who complete the entire pass.

anything on the purchased pass can only be earned through the pass, and once the season is over, will be unobtainable.

The first major example of this was seen in *DOTA 2* in 2013. Since then, almost every F2P/mobile game will have some form of a battle pass purchase. A similar version but not as effective is the monthly resource pass. By buying it, consumers get free resources daily, but this is not tied to anything gameplay related. Cost-wise, a season pass typically is the price of either a month's subscription or buying an expansion to a game – $14.99 to $19.99 USD – but some games can price theirs higher or lower. For developers, battle passes offer a reoccurring and consistent monetization option for games. It allows them to focus upcoming content and provide new reasons for players to keep playing daily. For consumers, the battle pass is attractive as a way for people who do play a game constantly to get rewarded with a lot of content for one flat purchase as opposed to many smaller microtransactions. Also, completing the battle pass will pay out equal or more premium currency, rewarding paying players with more resources.

With that said, there are valid criticisms of battle passes. The only way to access the unique content on the battle pass is to buy it. Even if someone has premium currency or spent money on the game in the past, they will not be able to access this content without the battle pass purchase. An example of trying to force someone to spend money is when a game has a free battle pass, but many of

Figure 10.12

Good content generation in live service games is all about getting the most value out of them. For games that are expanded with story content or unique challenges, developers will often take that content and make it accessible forever. Some examples are *Azur Lane, Arknights*, and *Dead by Daylight* (pictured here). When the season is over, all the tomes are still accessible, with their challenges and story unlocks, minus their rift point rewards that went with the battle pass.

the levels on it for free players don't reward anything for reaching them. This is a blatant example of making an experience worse for someone who doesn't spend money.

The thrill of unlocking content through play is a powerful motivator, but it also creates a situation where players can be pressured to keep playing a game. Depending on the length of the season and what challenges are available, it can become difficult to unlock everything for a season without playing daily. If someone buys the battle pass but is unable to complete it within the time allotted, they have effectively lost money on the pass.

I can see this system working in a fairer way by using the passes as a pseudo expansion to the game (fig 10.12). Once someone buys the pass, it, along with the challenges and possible rewards, becomes permanently associated to the account. If someone wants to burn through the content immediately, or take their time, there is no long-term penalty for it.

Long-Tail Live Service

11.1 The Challenge of Retention

For the final design chapter of this book, I want to focus on what it's like to keep F2P/mobile games supported over the long run. While most developers will look at profits as the major metric to a game's success or the peak number of players, the most important metric to gauge a game's success and long-term viability is retention. Live service games need a healthy and growing community if they want to have a chance at surviving.

Back in Section 5.5, I talked about the three phases of playing a game in terms of onboarding, daily loop, and late game, and briefly mentioned that this also relates to your player base. With live service games, your community can be made up of casual, core, and hardcore players.

The casual players are the ones just starting out and have the least investment in your game. When they finish with the onboarding, they may still be unsure whether they're going to stick around. Casual players are also the ones with the smallest chance of spending money regularly in your game. For games that feature new player's discounts and purchases, they may buy those if they are priced cheap enough.

DOI: 10.1201/9781003265115-11

Core players are the ones who have made it through the tutorials and are now playing your game daily. They know enough about the game now that they are willing to stick around and play (fig 11.1). There is a good chance that they will buy content meant to give them a boost if they're thinking about committing to the game or see a good deal.

The hardcore players are the ones who are playing your game at the late game. They have mastered the systems, they know how to play, and their goal is to either become the best players or see/collect everything the game has to offer. For this group, their purchasing becomes far more focused compared to the other two. They are only interested in things that they need or don't have. They will not spend on repeated banners, provided they already have that content, but will often spend more on something they don't have to complete their collection. The fans of these games may also spend money from time to time for the purpose of supporting a game they really like. This is the group that has the biggest potential of becoming whales for a game. In terms of the community, the hardcore group is where you'll receive the most feedback from, and your game may develop a YouTuber and streamer community from them.

As the designer, when you are thinking about long-term support and development, it is the hardcore group that will be your primary focus. Earlier in the book I said that you need to launch your game with the onboarding and daily loop

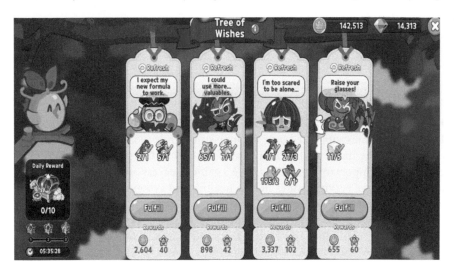

Figure 11.1

The daily loop always differs based on the game and gameplay systems in question. There is far more that goes into an effective daily loop than you might think. With *Cookie Run: Kingdom*, the only part of this daily challenge that is related to the gameplay has to do with the kingdom management, not any of the actual combat or other modes. You still need to do this system to unlock resources for progressing, but it is a rare example of a mobile game where not every system is attached to the daily loop play.

phases done, and the late game at least sketched out. Once your game is established, you are going to be spending most of your time creating new late game and purchasable content. With that said, even though your focus is going to be on the hardcore group, a healthy live service game needs people from all three groups to really succeed.

Without a hardcore following, there will be no one interested in the late game content. From a community standpoint, it will be harder to get the word out or give people something to aim for without hardcore players. Most people are not going to be playing any F2P/mobile game at the extreme levels but having people there and showing them how it's done is a popular driver in fan interest. If your game has nothing but hardcore players and no one else is joining, then your game's profits are completely held to how many players you have left. For each one that leaves that is not replaced, that is a permanent loss of your revenue (fig 11.2).

The core audience is needed to act as both a middle ground between the casual and hardcore, and to hopefully become hardcore players of your game if given enough time. For games that have a competitive focus, you need a core group of players to act as a buffer between the casual and hardcore audiences, as neither group gets any benefit out of PvP modes if they interact with one another. Casual players who get crushed by hardcore players will become frustrated and leave, while hardcore players who are looking for a challenge will get bored and not want to play.

Figure 11.2

A game that is only populated by hardcore players is often the sign that it does not have a future in the space. *Evolve* was a very original take on multiplayer design, but the high initial cost, high skill ceiling, and additional purchases kept a lot of people from playing it. The people who stuck around did end up enjoying the game, but without growth, there was not enough money coming in to justify continued development.

And you need to have casual players coming in to keep your fanbase growing. Without casual players coming in, you're never going to get more people to move through the game and become core and hardcore members. Failing to retain casual players is often the sign of a major problem with the game itself and is why making sure your onboarding is as good as possible is vital.

For a game to be considered successful in terms of its fanbase, you need to have players moving through all three groups. New casual players who are interested to learn your game, to then becoming core fans once they enjoy it, to finally becoming hardcore and more willing to stay and support you. The reason why developers focus so much on the onboarding and daily loop phase is that these are the times where people haven't decided to commit. Just because someone becomes a core fan doesn't mean they're automatically going to keep playing and become a part of your hardcore group. There are going to be core fans who like the game enough to keep playing, but not enough that they're going to commit and become hardcore. Likewise, they may also find themselves losing interest for any reason and stop playing. Therefore, all three groups are required and why you can't rely on just any one group if you expect your game to succeed long term.

Having a healthy community and keeping people invested can also lead to more word of mouth and the pop culture effect I'm going to talk about in Section 11.5.

11.2 The Two Kinds of Content

Long-term support of a game is about the unending pursuit of new content. No matter how big your game is on day one, it will never be enough to satisfy players. In Section 11.6, I'm going to talk about what new content means to the player base and how to capitalize on it.

There are two broad categories of content. The first kind is designed content, or content developed by the design team. This includes, but is not limited to, new maps, new characters, cosmetics, events – anything from the team that becomes official content for the game (fig 11.3).

The second kind is player-generated, or user-generated, content and represents what the player base brings to the game. For any game with modding support, players can create or install mods that can change the game in a variety of ways. Because mods are not officially supported by the designers, they are not considered official content in the game. For any competitive title, it is important to monitor what mods are being used in case someone made a mod that provides a competitive edge. The more important value that the player base brings is when it comes to multiplayer titles. As I've said, having a community is vital for any multiplayer-based game. In this capacity, other players provide content both directly and indirectly to the game.

In cooperative and competitive games, other players are required if you want to experience the game. In this capacity, the content they directly add becomes the lifeblood of a title, or the reason why it does not take off. The indirect content they provide comes from the impact they have on other players. When people

Figure 11.3

Any live service game will always have new designed content put into it, no matter how multiplayer-focused it may be. Depending on the game in question, this content may or may not be monetized. In *Street Fighter 5* (released in 2016 by Capcom), while new characters were monetized, all balancing and character updates were simply integrated into the game, as they should be. Putting fixes and balance patches behind a paywall is always a huge mistake.

watch a streamer or YouTuber playing a new game or showing off high-level play, it gets people engaged with the game. There are countless videos and streams dedicated to watching people open loot boxes or do gachas, as well as playing competitive games. They can also provide indirect content as being the top player and either a goal to reach or someone to beat and take the crown. In the previous section talking about converting core players to your hardcore base, seeing the top players, and trying to get to that level is a popular motivator for competitive games (fig 11.4). On the social side, any game that gives the player a creative space to do what they want to lets the community engage with each other without competing. We can see this in a lot of low-stakes games as well, such as *Animal Crossing: New Horizons* by Nintendo and released in 2020.

With both groups of content, there is a circular nature to interaction. Releasing new content will keep people interested in your game and provide a title with player-generated content and hopefully revenue, which that interest creates the need for the designers to create more content. This feedback loop is the inherent goal of all live service games – to put out content that brings in enough money to fund the studio to afford creating more content and repeat.

For the rest of this section, I want to focus on the content created by the developers, as this is what you have direct control over. Live service games differ from traditional games in the way that they need to get the most value out of content

Figure 11.4

For games that develop a competitive/Esports following, watching grandmaster play of these games not only drives consumer interest, but earns the game more money and clout in advertising and major tournaments, such as *DOTA 2*'s world championship known as "The International." A competitive game with a healthy Esports scene can remain relevant just on the prestige and following of the major players/teams alone.

developed. You must look at your content as a way of driving interest to your game, and that means developing content that works with your core gameplay loop and your monetization models.

If your game is about competing with other players, then first and foremost, content must be created to keep that engaging. For a game like *Dead by Daylight*, that means adding in new characters to shake up matches. However, a big aspect of playing *DBD* is having different maps with their own layouts, so there must be a focus on creating new maps. And of course, cosmetics for every character is a third area that has content developed for it. If your game is about playing as different characters, such as a MOBA or hero collector, then obviously you are going to have to keep coming up with new characters and accompanying cosmetics to go with them.

You want to avoid content that is "one and done" – something that after the player finishes it, they never have to do it again, but there is an exception. For games built on story-based design, creating new chapters of stories is an important part of development. The reason is that the story content is what people did as part of the daily loops and core gameplay, and for free players, this is often their source of free premium currency.

This is where one of the best examples of content you can add to your game come in: special events. Special events are limited-time pieces of content that are

Figure 11.5

Special events in live service games go beyond just having new characters or a new update. Depending on how far the designer wants to go, they can feature entirely new gameplay which can also be a way of getting feedback to see if it's worth continuing in future updates. With this event running in *Arknights*, there is a brand-new story, new hazards on maps, and a new sticker customization system. These events also lead to a short-term focus on playing them as opposed to the regular content.

only limited by your imagination (fig 11.5). Some games have seasonal events, monthly events, side stories, mini-games; there are no limits to limited-time events. These events always come with content unique to them, along with the chance of getting a variety of rewards. This can include exclusive characters, cosmetics, easy access to extra-rare resources, and more. As a huge example, while writing this book at the end of 2021, every mobile game I played to do research had an end of the year event. It's also common to have a half year anniversary to generate buzz. I'll discuss the importance of this more in Section 11.5.

Remember that the content you create for your game needs to be accessible for all players. If you're going to reward people for spending money during an event, then there needs to be free alternatives for the nonpaying players. You do not want to be seen as excluding members of your community from new content. For special events, they may have content grouped into different difficulties – one for casual and core players, and one for the hardcore, with more rewards given to the latter group for playing. Even though your hardcore fanbase will often be the focal point for new content developed, as the developer, you should always try to find ways to include casual and core groups with it. With *Azur Lane*, their events will frequently have mini-games and story content that anyone can experience regardless of their account level.

The last point for this section is designing original content – as in new systems or gameplay that is not in the game in any other form. For games that get into years of being supported, this is often the next step for them as a way of keeping interest and providing developers with a new area to create future content for. In the previous chapter with talking about third-generation games, *Warframe* is currently the best and biggest example of this with its multiple expansions. New content along these lines is a great way to create renewed interest in a game for fans, and maybe get some people who stopped playing to return to check it out. As I already said, you do not want to introduce new content that its only purpose is to reward people who spend money on your game. In *Marvel Strike Force*, the big additions to the game that came after launch was a battle pass system – or another monetization route and creating a new rarity power system that requires even more spending and luck for players to power up their characters. You can have content that can be attached to your monetization systems in some way, but you want to avoid creating new monetization systems after a game's release, as that can be viewed by consumers as demanding more money from your audience.

If you add in new forms of progression, or ways of powering up characters, that must be factored into any matchmaking systems and how players interact with each other. You don't want players who have access to a higher form of progression playing and competing against people who haven't gotten to them yet. This was the downfall of the game *Command and Conquer 4: Tiberian Twilight* released in 2010 by EA. A player's account level dictated what units and structures they could build when playing against other players. It was a common situation where a higher-level player could field units that the lower-level player had no counter against and would lose easily. This is again why developers who create new systems and additional content will not touch the onboarding and daily loop phases of the game once they have been set up.

11.3 Balancing Live Service Gameplay

Throughout this book I have talked about content and monetization, but it's time to talk about how this relates to progression and balance. Long-term support of a game means always thinking about what is next for your game, and what I'll be focusing on in Section 11.5.

Progression is about how the player grows in power and moves through the game. The two main ways are player-focused, as in the player becomes more accustomed to the game and plays it better, and character or abstracted-focused – getting better gear, leveling up, etc. For player-focused progression, there is always a limit both on the player and on the game itself. For action-based designs, developers must figure out the difficulty curve and what is required on the player's part to win. If someone cannot improve any further, then they are not going to be able to beat the game.

Abstracted progression is a popular option because it takes some of the slack off the player. If someone is not good at fast-paced dodging, they can just equip

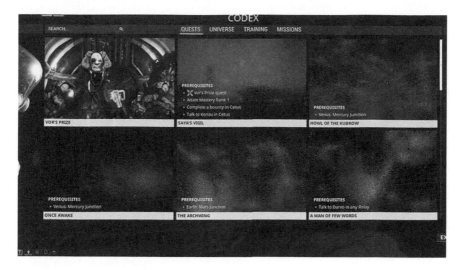

Figure 11.6

All the cosmetics, and even brand-new characters, in the world are not going to retain interest without having something to use them in. What is often the nail in the coffin for F2P/mobile games is focusing too much on the monetization systems, and not enough on new content to keep their playerbase interested. Warframe's quests provide a focus path through the content, while the expansions add in new challenges and systems for players to test their builds and warframes in.

better armor or level up to compensate. The beauty of abstracted progression from a designer's point of view – particularly live service – is that you have an infinite pool of numbers to keep raising stats and create content. Most MMOGs will add more levels to their max level through expansions to give that continued sense of growth. The problem is that changing numbers is only a short-term fix and is not really affecting what it is like to play the game. Hitting a monster for 50 points of damage or 5,000,000,000 doesn't change the interaction in of itself.

For live service games, it is far better for monetization purposes to introduce content that changes the gameplay. New warframes in *Warframe*, new characters in *Dead by Daylight*, all the new maps, modes, and items added to *Team Fortress 2*, and the list goes on. While cosmetics are popular as I have talked about, it's new gameplay content that will drive and retain player interest in your game (fig 11.6). However, this is where a lot of problems can happen depending on the design of your game.

PvE games have it a little easier since there is no competition going on. For PvE, you need to balance added content with what is currently accessible by your players. For games with randomized progression, such as ARPGs or gacha-focused, you need to examine what the average skill and abstracted levels of your audience are. If you release content that only the top 10% of your players have any hope of clearing, you are going to alienate a lot of your audience. You want to weigh the difficulty of the new content with the free or guaranteed options that a player has. The reason why is that these categories are the baselines of what every

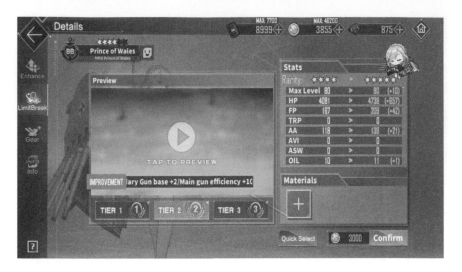

Figure 11.7

Promoting characters in gacha-styled games is a popular system that greatly extends the progression curve and monetization options, as players will want their favorite characters to be as strong as possible. In *Azur Lane*, characters need to be promoted, or "limit broken" to keep leveling them so that they can adequately fight in the late game.

player of a game will have power-wise. When content is added that pushes stats further, you need to provide means for players to continue growing in power.

PvP games on the other hand are far more complicated. When players are competing, they will be looking at any and every advantage. As I talked about when it comes to ethical design, you cannot just keep selling power to create an arms race scenario. And to make matters even harder, added content must still be balanced compared to what is currently available. If a new character or card is simply better in every way to all your other content, the haves will love it and the have-nots will hate your game.

When I discussed hero collector games and how they often let players upgrade characters with copies pulled from their gachas, it is important to talk briefly about this. Many games use this as the primary form of pushing characters up their power curves. I find this system close to the concept of complete gachas that reward the player with the "best pull" only if they can complete a set. In this case, getting a rare character is not enough, you need multiple copies or suitable resources to get them to their strongest. If you are going to do this, then you need to offer players a free alternative, such as *Azur Lane* that has a general currency for upgrading characters besides the duplicates (fig 11.7).

Hero collector games will use rarity to define the power of characters in one of two ways. The first kind is that rarity equals power – a one-star unit will never be able to compete with a six-star. This has the effect of pushing players up the rarity system if they want to have any chance at playing the game. In *Marvel Contest of Champions*, there are duplicate versions of its characters at the different star rarities. Getting a good five- or six-star unit can mean the differences of easily completing content or having a tough time. This system can be restrictive and creates a rigid hierarchy for choosing characters.

Other games will keep the starting rarity levels smaller, perhaps only three, but allow the player to upgrade any character far beyond that. Even though the rarest tier will have great abilities and be viable, someone can upgrade lower tiers to the point that they can compete stat-wise with the higher. In this way, the hierarchy is more fluid, with strategies built around certain combinations as opposed to whoever has the highest rarity automatically wins. This is also balanced around the fact that the resources needed to upgrade lower rarity units is easier and cheaper to get. While the higher-tiered units will have more utility, the higher stats on lower units should still allow them to make progress.

From a design standpoint, it is more interesting and healthier for your gameplay to avoid raw power as a form of progression. What makes games like deck builders or party-based RPGs so interesting to play is the concept of producing different strategies based on the options at hand. Here is a quick example, let's pretend that we have two cards in a deck builder:

Card 1:

- Health – 2
- Damage – 3
- Cost – 2

Card 2:

- Health – 2
- Damage – 4
- Cost – 1

Without any other details to these cards, there is never a reason someone should ever have card 1 in their deck once they get card 2. What you want to look at when it comes to designing content are interesting new mechanics or ways to play without needing to raise stats. Let us try this with the cards:

Card 1:

- Health – 2
- Damage – 3
- Cost – 2
- Special effect – if there are any water creatures adjacent to this card, +1 health and damage

Figure 11.8

It is always assumed in games with rarity tiers that the higher ones are inherently better, but power by itself only provides a short-term benefit. With *Arknights* the five and six-star characters will often share roles and base functionality with lower-tier units, but they will always have something exclusive to them that drives their value up. This character summons helpers like other operators, but her summons are different from the other summoners.

Card 2:

- Health – 2
- Damage – 4
- Cost – 1
- Special effect – for each turn this card remains on the field, lose 1 point of damage

With these changes, these cards now have different purposes and utility. More importantly, card #2 does not immediately replace card #1 in terms of value. This point is important to understand as a designer when releasing content, you never want added content to simply be the better version of old content (fig 11.8). You want to provide players with as many interesting, different, and viable ways to play your game. This leads to a healthier game, and one where the meta is not set in stone.

For live service games that are built on new characters, part of the balancing challenge is how this relates to your monetization system. Again, you need to create content that will entice people to spend, but at the same time, it can't become required. A problem seen in a lot of F2P/mobile games is that a player's ability to keep playing using the free content becomes less and less the further they get into the game. Remember my point about PFD – someone should be able to compete without spending money. This is also where the difficulties of adjusting the metagame come in that I talked about in Section 7.2. People will become frustrated if every added content update brings with it a new advantage for paying players.

With that said, it is time to talk about updating content. There is always the possibility that no matter how much you playtest something, that when it gets out into the general game it will be imbalanced for one reason or another. Incidentally, this is why coming up with unique rules or mechanics for new content can backfire in a sense, as that content is a lot harder to gauge in terms of its effectiveness. Here is an example from *Marvel Strike Force*. One of the characters that was added in had the unique power to revive a defeated member of their team using their ultimate skill. By itself, this is a neat ability that no one else had access to. However, when this is combined with characters that synergize with other members of the team, it can become a nightmare to fight when a player kills an important teammate to only have them revive the very next turn. Coupled with the time-limit matches for PvP, and this character provides a huge advantage.

When a situation like this happens, as the designer, you should first look at how powerful an option is. If the player uses X, is it an automatic win with no workaround? If something is successful, but only under specific conditions, then it can be fair to have something that works if the player can pull it off (fig 11.9).

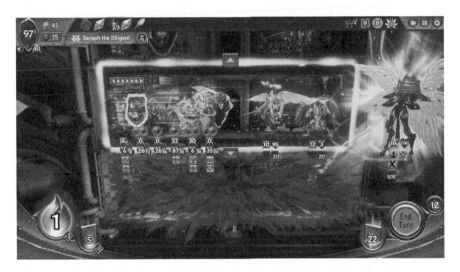

Figure 11.9

At the heart of the design of roguelikes (or any game with different ways to play) is coming up with viable strategies and figuring out how they should be balanced. In this scene from *Monster Train*, I used a frostbite build that continues to build and causes damage each turn to beat the final boss. There is no one perfect build in the game, it all comes down to building the right combination of cards and artifacts to capitalize on a strategy. If the entire game becomes a joke due to one option, or a set of options, then that may be worth looking at in terms of balance.

However, if the condition is so easy to do and that it wins every time, then there is a problem. The next detail is that you need to look at ways of dealing with it. If you cannot come up with any suitable answers, then it's time to either make other options better or make that option worse.

A quick example of a situation like this happened to *Hearthstone* in its first year. There are always distinctive styles of playing the different deck types in the game, and for a time the most powerful option was something called "Miracle Rogue." The strategy was to use a specific card that allowed the rogue to keep pulling cards out of their deck along with another card that lowers the cost of the next card played that turn, to allow someone to keep playing and drawing cards for far longer than anyone else. In a card-based game, the more cards in your hand gives you more options and control over the match. The problem with this strategy was that it was too easy to do, could not be easily countered by the opposing player, and guaranteed an advantage for the rogue.

It is always better to figure out ways of leaving great abilities alone and boosting the other options, as opposed to reducing it down to everything else. Keep in mind that when a situation like this happens, you must produce an answer for it. What Blizzard did was raise the cost of the card that started the combo which made it harder to produce the same results from happening. With *Marvel Strike Force* they messed up in two ways: they simply made the character harder to get – incentivizing spending and punishing those that did not have them. And second, they eventually added a new mechanic that counters revives, but it was only on a legendary character that free players had a tough time getting.

For any added content that creates new mechanics or rules for the game, there must always be a free option that can compete with it. The last example is not how you want to go about balancing your game. You do not want to introduce imbalanced problems in your game and then sell players the solution to them. The best content to put into a game is not something that has no equal, but something that creates another choice or way to play your game. You can also add more complicated mechanics and rules onto rarer cards and characters, so that the act of acquiring it does not automatically mean that the player is instantly more powerful. A general rule of thumb to keep in mind is that the more complicated or harder it is to do something, the stronger that option should be as a reward for players who can pull it off.

Returning to games like *Team Fortress 2* and *Dead by Daylight* that deal with unique characters and what I talked about in Section 8.5. Both games have definitive lists in terms of how complicated certain characters are to play. Outside of the hardcore players, most people are not going to master, or even like, every single character, and that is okay. The goal of the design team is to create a diverse pool of options so that there is at least one playstyle represented for every person playing.

11.4 Pop Culture Promotion

The longer a live service game is out and doing well affords it unique advantages compared to retail games. When you have a game that people are playing

Figure 11.10

Collab events are popular among gacha games as a way of getting recognized properties and their characters as playable versions in the respective game. In this event from *Alchemy Stars*, it is featuring a collab with the anime/manga *Miss Kobayashi's Dragon Maid*. There will often be a side story also created for the event about how these characters are represented in the world of the game.

regularly to the point that it becomes a part of daily life, that game begins to grow beyond just the game market. Successes like *Fortnite*, *Among Us*, and some of the larger mobile games, start to be mentioned outside of the games and the culture itself. With *Fortnite*, the dances in the game started to be done on major networks, and there have been movie premieres and music concerts put on within the game. *Among Us* had a stream featuring notable politician Alexandria Ocasio-Cortez and other famous streamers playing together.

When this happens with a game, more opportunities present themselves in another money-making gold mine: collab events. Collaborations between different properties can be a lucrative deal for everyone involved. How it works is that the game in question will get access to the IP of another property to make content that fits within the gameplay (fig 11.10). Contract negotiations are private to the parties involved, which makes it hard to outline how this works specifically. I can assume that the licensee will receive an upfront cost and/or sharing the revenue for their content purchased while it is available. Depending on the licensee, they may put in demands based on how their content will be depicted in a game.

The actual use of the property depends on the game in question. For hero collectors, this can be creating a character based off another property and putting them into the game. Gacha games use this formula to create limited exclusive characters that can drive up their value far greater compared to other created characters. A popular option is to create collab-based cosmetics, such as IP-specific skins or cosmetic items. *Fortnite* has featured multiple collabs with everything from Marvel, DC, the Super Bowl, anime, cartoons, and even celebrities like Arianna Grande. *Dead by Daylight*, as I am drafting this book, has cornered the market on horror movie and game collabs, and has developed content based off properties like *Hellraiser, Halloween, Silent Hill*, and others. Collab events between different properties is a popular way of getting new fans to check out either property or energize current fans who are interested in the collab itself.

With that said, collabs bring with it their own unique hurdles for designers to deal with. When you are negotiating to get another property's IP, they may require specific demands from you. A popular one is that the IP cannot be seen doing something "off brand," like showing a character like Superman or Mickey Mouse doing violent acts. One detail that can lead to the collab backfiring is the duration of the deal itself. With any kind of licensing deal, the licensee has control over how long they grant the license to their property. There have been many video games removed from stores, or content removed from games, when the term of the original contract has run out and a new deal cannot be made. This gets into contract negotiations and IP law and is both beyond the scope of this book and outside of my knowledge base. One thing is clear in every situation, once someone has spent money on the content and they now own a copy of it, that specific content cannot be taken away from someone.

For cosmetic and limited-time events, this content is not changing the balance of the game. However, if we are talking about gameplay-effecting content, that's a different story. Collab events that also embrace FOMO as a part of their marketing strategy, which I talked about earlier, are an example of unethical monetization. For collabs that bring gameplay-effecting content, you need to be incredibly careful about the terms of the deal.

A straightforward way to anger your fanbase is to have content that has gameplay to it, and then having the license run out and that content is no longer available. When this happens, you need to have contingency plans in place for the community. Due to how contracts are drafted, developers will often know well in advance when a license is going to run out. You need to inform the community and make it as transparent as possible what is going to happen to that content. Some games will drastically lower the price of the DLC to get as many people as possible to buy it before it can no longer be sold. If content came with something that has become part of the entire experience and the game's balancing has been affected because of it, then it is better to give that part away for free as opposed to altering the game. With *Dead by Daylight*, the developers lost the license to *Stranger Things* that brought with it new characters, new perks, and a new map. While people can no longer buy the characters or play on the map, the perks that were designed for those characters are now accessible to every player whether they bought the content or not.

Having your own IP become popular enough to be licensed to other games is not something you can really plan around. Companies are looking for two

Figure 11.11

Fortnite is a good example of a property well suited to collaborations. While it does have its own internal rules and lore surrounding the major events, none of that is attached to the actual playing of the game. Since skins don't bring with them any gameplay advantages, there is no dissonance created from all these properties intersecting with each other. However, tying collabs like this to one-time events is a clear example of exploiting FOMO.

things: something that works well with their IP, and something that is extremely popular. The other and simpler option is to throw money at the licensee you are trying to court, but that requires having access to a lot of money to begin with. With a game like *Fortnite* or *Fall Guys,* which does not have strict rules for their content, anything and everything can be put into them (fig 11.11). For games with a more hardcore audience, they may not like it if you are putting in brands that do not fit the universe and view it as a blatant cash grab.

The strategy of taking characters and brands outside of their respective universe and market is a trend that has grown more popular over the 2000s and 2010s. What originally started as a popular fantasy book series, *The Witcher,* by Andrzej Sapkowski has since become a successful game series by CD Projekt Red, the basis for the CCG *Gwent* (released in 2017 by CD Projekt Red), and a series on Netflix. The same could absolutely be said of the entire *The Lord of the Rings* franchise by J.R.R. Tolkien. Even if the property itself may not be seen at first as being transferable, it can lead to opportunities and content that grows it even further than before, as I mentioned with *League of Legends* in Section 2.3. Animated series and music releases have become two popular routes for games, with both *Arknights* and *Azur Lane* having them.

Having your game reach the same level of awareness as the other properties mentioned in this section will take time. When they work, they can give a property a huge boost that can be continued with additional collabs down the line.

For games to get to this point, they need to be successful and as the topic for the next section, properly supported.

11.5 Long-Term Support

For the F2P and mobile games that do become successes, the next step is shifting into long-term support of the title. This includes releasing new monetized content, fixing any bugs or complaints, and designing additional content meant to flesh out the entire game.

As I have spoken about throughout this book, live service games continue to be supported for as long as the developers can keep people engaged, and that means the work for developing these games is never finished. I already spoke about the kinds of content earlier in this chapter, and as the designer, you need to set a reliable schedule for content. The challenge is having content come consistently to keep the fanbase happy, but still giving it enough time to be developed, play tested, and make sure there are not any issues with it.

There is no set answer to this; some games release updates every few weeks, once a month, every quarter, it all depends on the content that is being developed and the size of the team (fig 11.12). For games built on gacha design, it is rare to see one that goes more than a month or two without introducing a new character or bringing back a preexisting banner. Ideally, there should be an event or additional content always running so that people aren't just playing the daily loop

Figure 11.12

Following the initial success of *Warframe,* Digital Extremes grew to a multi-studio company with several hundred employees and offices around the world. This has helped them create new content and continue to update the game, such as when they added in the city of Cetus in the "Plains of Eidolon" update.

Game Design Deep Dive

or late game. In games where content is far more gameplay-effecting, such as deck builders with new expansions, they may take longer. In Section 7.2 on PvP design, I talked about the dangers of having a fixed meta. For any competitive-focused game, content updates are essential for introducing changes to the meta to keep things varied. As I mentioned earlier, new story-based content and events are added regularly and is often the way that nonpaying players can earn premium currency by continuing to do that content.

Due to the amount of work that goes into these games, designers who release games in the eastern markets may wait at least a year or more before releasing their global version. This does two things: it lets them know if the game is even popular to begin with and worth translating, and it builds up a pool of content that can be translated and used for the global version. When it comes to content releases, you want to space them out as to not burn through them all fast. For consumers, they do not want to load up a game and find that there are three or more months of events and content happening all at once. This can easily overwhelm someone and dilutes the value of the content in the first place.

There is one risk to this that I want to talk about. This chapter has focused on content creation, but updates to the UI/UX and QOL improvements are a big part of supporting these games. It is exceedingly rare to see a live service game never getting UX improvements over its life span. A widespread practice for eastern first-developed games is to combine QOL updates with the content updates that they were originally released in and put those out for the global version on a schedule. The idea is that the developers do not want to be seen like they are favoring new fans by giving them an improved version first.

This is something that I cannot agree with as someone who studies UI/UX and gameplay for a living. Remember, fans of these games are intelligent enough to look up what other territories have in terms of support and content, especially YouTubers and streamers who cover them. If they see that their version has noticeable problems or is just worse to play than what other people have, these fans are going to quit rather than play an "inferior" version. Sometimes you can get people to come back and check out what is new, but most people once they quit a game will not look at it ever again. Of course, if a QOL feature is only related to content or systems that are not in the game yet, then you don't need to worry about it.

The beauty about live service games from a marketing standpoint is that they can use major updates as a marketing push for new, existing, and returning players. *Team Fortress 2* during its heyday would often put out previews of the upcoming update and turn it into a week-long event (fig 11.13). Each day, they would release a new update to the website to preview the changes that would be coming with the full patch, complete with in-universe news pieces and storytelling to go with it. Overkill Software with *Payday 2* went even further and had a once a year "mega event" that they would release brand new updates to the game daily for an entire week. *Fortnite* puts a lot of work into their seasonal storylines and completely change the map layout with each season and add in new things that can occur.

Figure 11.13

Valve may have been the first studio that embraced turning game updates into marketing events. These events for *Team Fortress 2* would come to embrace the community and allow them to influence it and future ones. For the "War" update, the class that killed more than the other received an exclusive item in the form of the "gunboats."

Another option is to have special "returning player" events meant to give players who stopped playing a reason to come back. For F2P/mobile games that are around for years, these events are a great way to welcome back players and provide them with a recap of the game and be rewarded for it. In terms of when to have these, there is no set rule, but a good time to do it is when your game has dramatically changed over time or introduced a brand-new game system and content. Earlier in the book, I brought up games that have half year and yearly anniversaries as an example.

When you have something big coming to your game, you want to put your marketing efforts in to get as many people interested in the game. These events often mean sales, free rewards for playing, and the excitement of experiencing something brand new to the game. Because of all that, major updates are also when a game can see an influx of people playing the game at once. While it is unlikely that all those people will stay around, this is the best chance for you to convert new players into potential long-term fans.

As I talked about in Section 11.2, while there will be people who will take their time in your game, there will always be those that will quickly go through everything and will demand more. You need to make sure that content is coming to the game and to inform consumers about this. One of the first things that will get added to a live service game after launch is fleshing out the late-game content. You should always launch with a system in place so that your core audience has

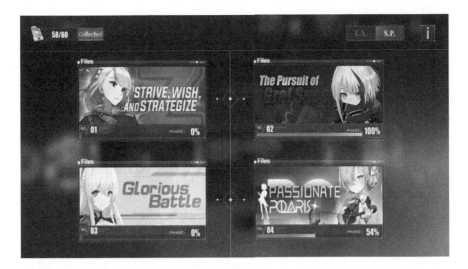

Figure 11.14

As I mentioned earlier, good content for a live service game should stay in it and helps bolster the number of things for players to do. *Azur Lane* will routinely take the story content from events and put them as free mini chapters for players to do for additional rewards or learning more about the world of the game.

something to do. Unfortunately, for developers, it does not matter what the quality of the game is at launch if there is not enough content to keep player interest.

For special or seasonal events, it is common to set a requirement in terms of who can participate in it. This is often restricted to the account level that people can access the daily loop phase of the game. One reason is to not overwhelm new players with content and systems while they are still learning everything else. As a common strategy, think of new content for your game as being self-contained – something that once it's released can stand on its own without connection to other content. You do not want to have content that is linked: someone must own or have done content A to access the newly released content B.

Games like *Azur Lane, Arknights*, and *Dead by Daylight* treat new story/free content or releases as "episodes" or "chapters" (fig 11.14). This is content that remains open year-round and can be experienced in any order. While *Warframe* will place new content based on the difficulty and complexity that it requires, which the game cleanly lays out for players on their progress page.

As a word of warning, long-term support of a game is both the life and death of a live service title. The second you announce that you are done releasing new content for a game, all growth of your community and fanbase will cease. If your game has any Esports connection, there is a good chance that tournaments may be pulled as well. This is one of the major investments for live service games, and why most studios that have a hit will continue to work on just the single game. In Section 4.6, I talked about why you want to avoid sequels for live service games, but that also means your studio becomes completely tethered to that one game, but for the successes of the third generation, that is the goal and not a problem.

11.6 When a Live Service Game Ends

Throughout this entire book, I have spoken about the good and bad of live service and F2P game design. The games that are good go on to be developed for years, and the bad ones are shut down. While it's easy to see why a bad game gets shut down, this can happen to good ones as well, and why I want to talk about this.

At the end of the day, a live service game that isn't making a profit will not be supported forever. A game needs to be making enough to cover the cost of development and maintaining its servers for online play. Some developers will try to right a sinking ship with new content, major marketing pushes, etc. Even the best live service games – the ones that won awards when they came out – can still eventually find themselves struggling or not in the limelight. *World of Warcraft* is a game that has certainly earned enough money to consider it a success, but its subscriber base has shrunk since its heyday. According to stats at the end of 2021, the game averages around 2.2 million subscribers, a stark difference from having over 10 million a month. While it is still one of the most played MMOGs today, *Final Fantasy 14* has, at this time, overtaken it in terms of monthly subscribers.

Depending on the resources of the studio, they may continue to passively support a F2P game; this is known as putting a game on "maintenance" (fig 11.15). What that means is that the game will not receive any more content updates; it is effectively finished in terms of development. Consumers can still spend money in the game if they would like, or content may just be made free depending on the game. The only support that a game like this will continue to get are bug fixes and maintaining the servers for online play. In this way, even though the game will not be going on to becoming a massive hit, it can keep the fanbase happy and may still generate some income to balance out the maintenance cost.

If that is not enough, a studio may consider shutting down a game completely. If they have decided to work on a sequel, a new F2P property, or the studio is going under, those are other reasons for shutting down an older F2P game. Games that are shut down this way will inform the consumer base at least a few months in advance to give people time to experience it one last time. As a way of saying "thank you" to the players, the developers will often turn off all monetization and just give players access to the best characters so that they can enjoy the game until the last day. For many MMOGs that have been shut off, developers and fans have staged grand events for the final day.

How a live service game ends will determine the future of the studio in the space. Sometimes a game goes under not because it did anything unethical, but it just wasn't earning enough to maintain development. In some cases, a live service game may be shut off for development to shift to a new version or a completely new game by the developer. Sadly, there have also been F2P games released over the 2010s that were simply set up as a "slash and burn" affair without any real care

Figure 11.15

Heroes of the Storm (released in 2015) was Blizzard's attempt at entering the MOBA genre and having a game that combined all its properties under one banner. Despite attracting a fanbase, it did not come close to the successes of *DOTA 2* and *LOL*. Blizzard decided to put it into maintenance which also ended up killing the Esports tournament league around the game.

toward the longevity of the title or the studio. Consumers can tell when a company is doing what they can to support a game while not exploiting their fans. One of the more salient points about live service games is that when a game shuts down, all the microtransactions purchased cease to exist for the consumers.

Video game consumers have an exceptionally long memory when it comes to studios that have fleeced money out of their customers. If your live service game ends positively, you can often count on those fans and new ones supporting your next title. If it ends badly with a lot of angry consumers, you may find your studio blacklisted by consumers and word of mouth will spread fast to avoid your future projects.

As a final point for this section, when live service games are turned off, they become completely inaccessible to everyone. Returning to Section 2.4, much like the MMOG space, this has led to a lot of games that simply cease to exist in the industry. There have been pushes to create preservation servers and ways to play games that are no longer being supported this way, but it has been a tough legal battle to get the rights to do this. Several F2P and MMOGs have seen fan support this way, but I would personally like to see more developers and consumers take an interest in preserving games regardless of their overall success.

12

Looking Forward with Free-to-Play Design

12.1 The Future of the Market

At the end of each *Game Design Deep Dive*, I try to think about what the future will hold for the genre. For the F2P genre, this is a hard one to judge. As I talked about in Section 9.5, the danger of monetization laws being passed still looms over the industry, and there are plenty of people who are still put off by mobile design and abusive F2P monetization. One thing is for sure – the pitch from designers that "mobile gaming is the future of games" that the mobile industry and supporters liked to say in the early 2010s is over. While there are great mobile and F2P games with unique designs, as I spoke about regarding the third generation in Chapter 10, examples like *Warframe* and *Path of Exile* seem to be the exception to ethical design rather than the norm currently.

New mobile and F2P games are still being released every few months, but they are entering a space where consumers have seen all the monetization tricks already. The games that have succeeded are not going to go anywhere, and it's an ever increasingly harder uphill battle for new games (fig 12.1).

There is one route for these games to go, but it will require a lot of work, and that is going to the console and PC markets. As I said earlier in this book, popular

DOI: 10.1201/9781003265115-12

Figure 12.1

At the time of writing this book, the undisputed king of the gacha market is still *Genshin Impact*, which just released version 2.4 at the start of 2022, and no other second or third generation mobile game covered here comes close to beating it. The #2 game currently is *Uma Musume Pretty Derby* released by Cygames in 2021. There are competitors being developed, but are not available globally just yet.

mobile emulators like Bluestacks are available, but that is different from having an officially supported version. Digital stores like Steam, PSN (PlayStation Network), and others have been supporting F2P games over the 2010s. Of the many F2P games released on mobile, only a handful have been ported to other platforms, such as *Genshin Impact*. However, while more platforms do give a game a chance of getting a larger fanbase, there are several roadblocks with mobile games. Part of the attraction of being on mobile is that the Google Play Store and Apple Store let mobile developers do what they want in terms of monetization. Console and PC stores are stricter when it comes to monetization systems.

Being on PC presents a security issue for mobile developers. There are many hackers out there who can figure out how to crack a game for free currencies or to mess with the servers. And a developer using intrusive copy protection, such as what was reported that miHoYo supposedly did with the PC version of *Genshin Impact*,[1] can drive away consumers who don't trust certain security software. Whenever a game gets ported to another platform, that will require additional costs to make sure that the port not only works well but also plays to the new platform's strengths. One of the easiest ways that developers mess up when porting from mobile to PC or vice versa is not properly redesigning the UI and UX for the different control methods.

Another risk developers can take is expanding the servers or regions that can access their games. There are still plenty of successful mobile games that are limited to only a few regions. The greater the number of people who can access a game, the greater the chance of that game succeeding and finding a market. However, more regions also mean a greater cost in terms of supporting and maintaining those games. For titles that are built on specific cultural tastes and properties, their success may not translate to a different country.

Some of you reading this may be wondering if the industry is due for a fourth generation of mobile/F2P design, and there is the burgeoning start of something new as I am writing this book.

12.2 Play-to-Earn Design and NFTs

This section has the potential to be the most dated or controversial in terms of its information depending on when you are reading this book. A technology and monetization model that is currently being argued among developers and consumers is blockchain and "play-to-earn" design. I do not have the technical background to go fully into what a blockchain is or how it works, but its purpose for what I am talking about is to create a piece of digital content that is unique and cannot be easily replicated, if at all (fig 12.2). This content is referred to as a non-fungible token or commonly known as an **NFT**. When people talk about digital copies and ownership, content is designed to be easily reproduced as its just code. One of the major positives of the digital age is that there is no longer a shortage of any video game, as key to access it on any store can be generated far easier than creating physical media.

Figure 12.2

Ubisoft is the first major game studio to create a blockchain platform known as Quartz with NFTs called Digits. Unfortunately for them, it has been mocked by consumers and other developers and would be one of many examples of people trying to strike it rich without understanding the market.

With the use of blockchains and creating NFTs, developers are trying to recreate the concept known as play-to-earn. When MMOGs became huge in the late 1990s and players interacted with each other, these games would go on to have a virtual economy. Something is only worth what someone is willing to pay, and rare items, in-game currency, or even services conducted by players in the game, would have a real-world price tag to it. Many MMOG developers did not fully grasp what this meant or how to capitalize on it, and to avoid dealing with it, they made these activities against the rules and banned people from doing it.

Instead of stopping the behavior, it simply moved to the underground and ethically gray markets. With *World of Warcraft* and other MMOGs, the game's popularity and demand for the in-game currency "gold" created a market known as "gold farming." People would play the game all day with the explicit goal to generate as much gold as they could to then sell it on a third-party site to people who needed it. The buying and selling of virtual goods in any game that has them has been going on for decades now. This can even be traced to games today that have online goods without being MMOGs themselves, as I talked about in Section 6.4.

What developers and companies are looking to do is to create a legal form of virtual goods ownership that there cannot be any disputes over. The point of the NFT is that using the blockchain to generate it creates a unique piece of code. If a game or company creates, or "mints," 100 copies of something, those hundred copies are the only ones that exist for it. And in return, people who get those copies are free to use or sell them to others as they see fit, creating a new virtual economy.

To get money, consumers must sell their NFTs through a secure site, one example being Solonart. The transaction is based on whatever virtual currency a store uses, which can then be converted to a real-world currency. What developers get out of this is that for each time a transaction is done, they will earn residuals as part of the transaction fee for the purchase. On paper, this sounds like a tremendous step forward in terms of digital ownership. If this does play out, it could change the market for virtual goods around the world. However, there are several concerns that are currently being argued at the time of drafting this book.

First is the resources required to generate an NFT. The process to mint a new NFT requires far more computing power and energy compared to regular code. For the first NFTs created, the cost to the environment and energy to make them could have cost more than the value of the NFT itself. This led to a shortage of video cards and driving up the market for high-end PC cards in 2020 and 2021. The amount of power needed to run this has also led to environmental concerns. One of the more popular blockchains is Ethereum, with a newer one called Solana. At this time, there is work being done to create technology that can better refine the process for minting an NFT to make it less hardware and environmentally intensive.

The bigger problem is the negative stigma surrounding NFTs thanks to the first adopters. There are a lot of people and big companies jumping on NFTs, much in the same way the early mobile game gold rush occurred, to try to make as much money in as little time as possible. People who are buying and selling

Figure 12.3

Dead by Daylight gets one more mention in this book but not in a positive way. Following the release of their update featuring *Hellraiser*. Behavior Interactive announced that it would start selling models of their killers as NFTs. The idea received so much negative backlash from fans that they took down the entire project for now. And again, owning an image or an in-game model provides no real value to the item in question.

images as NFTs are missing the point. An image immediately loses its value when someone can just search for it on Google; it has no utility that would give it value and seems like a false positive for the purpose of NFTs in my opinion (fig 12.3).

For video game companies rushing to make a blockchain-based game, they are not really going into detail about the purpose of the NFTs in the game other than to make them more money. Ubisoft's blockchain platform and NFTs are set up currently for just in-game cosmetics. Just like with the fig 12.2 example, there is no utility or functionality to justify their use in-game. For studios that are talking about minting gameplay-effecting content, that also has a serious drawback. For these games, the NFTs once they are minted are fixed elements with no room to grow or change. That means, from a gameplay perspective, trying to play a game like this is going to be a poor experience because either nothing else comes close to those items, raising their value at the expense of being P2W, or added content will come out that's better, devaluing those NFTs and costing the owners their investment.

Some developers have spoken about the idea that eventually NFTs will be transferable between games, so that someone getting one in game A can bring it over and use it in game B. This idea sounds like it would not only create a P2W environment but would also be a nightmare from a balancing and development standpoint to have to consider other game content as part of your own design.

There is one exception to the problems with NFTs in games at the time of writing this book. A friend and colleague of mine, Ramin Shokrizade, who has been in the virtual economy space for over 20 years now, is making a game: *Project Eluüne*. The economy of the game is built entirely on players creating creatures, which are dynamic NFTs, and the ability for players to buy and sell them. Unlike what has been discussed in other games, the NFTs here can grow and change in diverse ways. What that means is that every creature will have their base value in terms of the stats designated by the developers, but also the value of the time and resources players put into them, and finally, creatures can grow and change. What that means is that there is an actual economy built on the usage and value of the content, as opposed to just passing static images around. Revenue will be based on subscription services players can subscribe to, and the residuals that are earned over transactions. This is the only NFT game that is being developed today where the developer is not selling or minting any gameplay-related NFTs, where these are minted by players from ingredients and cannot be purchased from the developer. I do not want to sound biased considering I know Ramin personally, but his game shows the best chances of succeeding as both a NFT game and a play-to-earn one. However, given the negative reaction and PR surrounding NFTs at this moment, it is going to be hard to build consumer trust.

Like the early claims of VR taking over the industry, I see the industry's approach to blockchains and NFTs at this time being something whose importance could transcend the game industry with the technology. The idea of digital ownership is something that has been in the back of minds since the world went digital. With the growth of Steam and other digital platforms, they have always stated that consumers do not own the games they buy but the "license" to play the game on their platform of choice. This has also led to consumers unable to sell games they do not want on digital platforms. With the functionality of blockchains and NFTs, it could lead to a new way of owning, buying, and selling digital content. Many mobile games are all about the player accumulating vast amounts of resources or duplicate copies of content that they have no use for. Imagine if someone could take their copy of a UR character and sell it based on an established market price, with the consumers and developers profiting from it.

As for my own thoughts on the matter, just like with F2P design, mechanics and systems are not inherently good or evil, but it's how they are used. For the people and companies who are rushing onto the model hoping to strike it rich, it is again like the early adopters who rushed onto mobile with exploitative games and poisoned the market because of it. And for each one of them that tries and fails is going to make it that much harder for any ethical uses of blockchain to be noticed. If history repeats itself, I'm predicting the first generation of blockchain and NFT games to fail due to not understanding the potential of the space, and the developers who stick with it and prove its usefulness to have a chance to succeed after an uphill battle in the space.

Figure 12.4

For this final chapter all of you get an Ultra-Rare image of the "Joshboxes" I made to promote Game-Wisdom.

12.3 Conclusion

This has been one of the largest topics I have written about when it comes to game design (fig 12.4). This is a genre that I both love and hate. Seeing games that do well and are rewarded with months and years of support is a wonderful thing. But when developers purposely make exploitative content, and it works, it cheapens the industry and makes it harder for other games to succeed.

While doing research for this book, I was dismayed that there were not more positive examples of F2P games to talk about. Most of the mobile games I spent time in, even the better examples, still made use of unethical practices. That is what worries me about the market, that these practices are no longer being called out or punished but are normalized among developers and considered par for the course among consumers. While many consumers are quick to point out egregious examples of P2W and unethical design, far too few understand the subtler aspects that go into making these games dangerously addictive.

That was the other reason for authoring this book: to expose the tricks and psychological aspects that go into monetization systems. The more people that are educated on them, the less likely they are going to continue working. In turn, it will force developers to look at other, hopefully more ethical, means of monetizing their games. I want the notion of player-friendly design to become the standard of F2P and live service games, and that's going to be difficult. There is not one F2P/mobile game on the market at the time of writing this, not even

Team Fortress 2, Path of Exile, or *Warframe*, that perfectly hits all four points I laid out earlier in this book.

With the market, there is no way that it will crash from a lack of consumer interest, as F2P and mobile games have the largest market today. But between abusive monetization and developers trying to exploit NFTs and pay to earn gameplay, if things go too far and governments step in, a lot of companies are going to go under.

Lastly, I hope that every one of you reading this will take away this point – that game mechanics and systems are not inherently good, bad, or ugly. It is possible to create an ethical example of F2P design, but you must go into it realizing that you are not going to be making the same profits as those that exploit it. However, you will end up with a far healthier fanbase that will be willing to support you now and into the future.

The game industry has fully embraced the digital age and continues to be at the forefront of technologies and systems. While there are plenty of people joking about the failures in the NFT market, the impact that this could have in a few years' time could change the way we approach digital content, just as mobile games changed the market and awareness of video games forever.

Note

1. https://www.pcgamer.com/genshin-impacts-kernel-level-anti-cheat-no-longer-runs-after-you-close-the-game/

Glossary

AAA: A way of defining major studios in the game industry.

Aesthetics: The mood or feeling that is being conveyed by the game's art, sound, and UI/UX.

ARPG: Stands for action role-playing game and is a subgenre of RPGs that focus on real-time movement and combat and is more reflex based than traditional RPGs.

Avatar: A character controlled by the player in a video game that is often personalized to reflect the player.

CCG: Short for "collectible card game," a game that is played between people with decks of cards.

Clones: Used to label games that are copying a much more popular game in terms of its gameplay, aesthetics, or both. Depending on the level of copying, may be considered infringing on the copyright of another game.

Core gameplay loop: The primary gameplay system for each video game; the reason why someone is playing a game in the first place.

DLC: Stands for "downloadable content" and represents major pieces of content that are either added for free to a game or require a purchase to unlock.

Esports: Video games that are played as competitive sports, with teams, sponsors, and tournaments around the world.

ESRB: Stands for "Entertainment Software Ratings Board," a regulatory independent body established by the game industry to monitor and rate games based on their content and how the industry advertises games.

Free-to-play (F2P): A game genre that is known for having no upfront cost to play and earns its money through smaller purchases or microtransactions.

FOMO: Short for "fear of missing out." A marketing strategy used to make an offer more attractive by stating that once the promotion is over, the offer is gone forever.

Gacha: A popular monetization system seen in F2P and mobile games based on the capsule games known as "gachapon" in Japan. Consumers get a variety of prizes, but there is always a standout one that is the hardest and rarest to get.

Guilds: Can also be called alliances among other names. A group of players that team up under a single organization to share in rewards, complete specialized content, or fight other guilds for power and resources in a game.

IP: Short for "intellectual property" is a catch-all term for any property created that is not physical by nature. For video games, this includes, but not limited to, brands, studio names and works, and characters for a game.

Itemization: A way of describing the balance and design of items in a game that are meant to have an impact on the gameplay.

Live service: A form of game development that is about continually updating a game with new content and work for months and years after its initial release. It can also be referenced as "games as a service."

Loot box: A form of monetization where the consumer spends money to open a box and acquire random rewards with the chance of getting something rare.

Mechanic: A way to describe the actions or "verbs" that the player can do in a video game. Example: being able to jump in a video game would be a jumping mechanic.

Metagame: Used to discuss the popular options in a game at the current time and will change based on new content or updates added.

Microtransaction: A purchase made in a video game that is not related to the actual purchase of a video game. Despite the name, microtransactions can be quite expensive depending on the nature or purpose of the purchase.

MMOG: Stands for "massively multiplayer online game." A genre known for having huge numbers of players actively playing at one time on one or many servers.

MOBA: Stands for "multiplayer online battle arena." A type of game where players team up while controlling individualized characters to fight against an opposing team.

Mods: Content created by modders and added to a video game not by the original designers. A mod can change a video game in any number of ways based on the mod itself.

Modders: Someone who creates and uploads mods for video games.

Monetization: Used to describe systems in games that exist for the sole purpose of making money off consumers.

MUD: Short for "multi-user dungeon," an early form of the MMOG genre, players could connect to the game, interact with other users, and do a variety of things based on the game itself.

NFT: Short for "nonfungible token," a piece of content created using a blockchain to create something that is unique and not easily copied.

Pay to win (P2W): A term used to define a game where spending money provides an unfair advantage compared to people who don't spend or don't spend enough compared to their peers.

Pain point: A term to describe anything that happens in the user experience that makes a game worse for someone to play.

Personalization: The ability to change the appearance of a character without changing the gameplay.

Player-generated content: The ways in which someone playing a game directly or indirectly provides content to the game itself.

Player-friendly design: Also known as PFD, a term to describe games that are ethical in their monetization systems.

Premium currency: An in-game resource popularized by free-to-play games; it can only be earned by spending money and can be used to make playing the game easier in a variety of ways.

Procedural generation: A form of content generation when the game itself will generate something based on previously defined rules and elements by the designer and set up in an algorithm.

PvE: Stands for "player vs. environment" and denotes games with a focus on players fighting against computer opponents instead of each other.

PvP: Stands for "player vs. player" and denotes games that have a focus on players fighting against each other.

Quality-of-life: Features in a game that makes it easier/better to play without directly adding content to it.

RPG: Short for "role-playing game," a type of game that focuses more on leveling up characters and growing in power as opposed to twitch or reflex-based gameplay.

Skill ceiling: To describe how much skill is required by the player to beat the game.

Streamer: Someone who earns a living by streaming themselves via a platform like Twitch or YouTube.

Systems: A way to categorize similar mechanics in a game together that all serve the same purpose.

TCG: Short for "trading card game," a type of game that is played by collecting cards and building a deck to play against other players.

UI: Short for "user interface" and represents the way someone interacts with a video game using the on-screen elements and control inputs.

UX: Short for "user experience," and is a catch-all term for all the ways someone experiences a game and what affects them both positively and negatively.

Whale: A category of consumer coined by the gambling industry to describe someone who spends vast amounts of money and is often sought after by casinos and F2P games.

Index